IT'S ABOUT
CREATIVITY
DISCIPLINE
INGENUITY
SIMPLICITY
FORM
FUNCTION
SPACE
RESOLUTION
LAYERS
TEXTURE
COLOUR
BALANCE
+ RESULTS

THE LANDSCAPE ARCHITECTURE
OF PAUL SANGHA

THE LANDSCAPE ARCHITECTURE
OF PAUL SANGHA

WRITTEN BY
CAROLYN DEUSCHLE

ESSAY BY
BYRON HAWES

EDITED BY
OSCAR RIERA OJEDA

PRINCIPAL PHOTOGRAPHY BY
NIC LEHOUX

OSCAR RIERA OJEDA
PUBLISHERS

CONTENTS

THE LANDSCAPE ARCHITECTURE OF PAUL SANGHA

BY CAROLYN DEUSCHLE

To move through one of Paul Sangha Landscape Architecture's landscapes is to feel. The current of enchantment, the prick of surprise, and the softness of contemplation. There is an endless distance between humans and the landscape. In the impossible effort to twin them, their division is clarified. Still the desire burns to feel reconciled with the pulse that unites them. In this numinous territory, design works ceaselessly as a beacon calling landscape to our shore.

Works by Paul Sangha embrace moments when we are convinced of this coupling. The firm's designs are elegant, seductive, nimble and deceptively simple. Though the works are rigorous, the designs look effortless.

Paul Sangha gardens make nature a space for living. An evolution of the house, they complement and supplement the architecture by accentuating its design and conversing with it through landscape. In Paul Sangha's designs, the house and the garden are perceived in unison, as if one could not exist without the other. The garden makes the house sing, but it also has a song of its own.

A balance of slow and fast, steady and staccato is maintained as one walks the gardens. Paving patterns instill this cadence. Yet when there is something to be observed, like a flower, fountain, sculpture, or view, the rhythm begins to dissipate and the walk slows down. The choreography of movement controls the user's circulation and kindles a feeling of fluid progression through the landscape.

Design devices, like foils or points of interest, guide the eye through a sequence of visual scenes, which are carefully curated to allow depth and complexity. Paul Sangha works closely with artists and craftspeople to bring sculpture, art, and other works into the garden that both encourage one to stop and look and define spaces. The designs entrap the eye—drawing it in, releasing it, then drawing it in again—keeping the user curious, attentive, and compelled to keep exploring.

The natural scenery of the urban landscape in Vancouver, where many of the landscape architect's projects reside, is spectacular: Snow-capped mountains sweep the horizon, extreme ocean tides mark the passage of time and temperate climes nourish a robust ecosystem. The backdrop of nearly any view in Vancouver is a visual feast. Paul Sangha's designs incorporate the grandeur of the setting while delivering an experience compelling enough to bring your awareness to the immediacy of the garden. Yet the gardens do not compete with the view, nor the view with the gardens. They dance together with a potent choreography, the garden and the view giving way to each other's solo performances and improvisations and adding further dimensions to the landscape when considered as a whole.

However, the garden is always in the foreground of daily life; whether when walking the grounds, eating a meal outside, or simply looking out a window; the garden is both an object of pleasing beauty and a facilitator of transformations, the kind that come hand-in-hand with a closeness to nature.

During the design phase, Paul Sangha seeks to understand the site—its physical and sensorial qualities, the palimpsest of former owners, ecological demands; the client—the pace and behaviors of their daily lives, their desires, needs, and understandings of the spaces that surround them; and the architecture—its relationship with the landscape and the potential for this relationship to be deepened. The firm garners client trust—which allows for creative freedom—by quickly gleaning the client's wishes and articulating them back through words and conceptual drawings. They work with humility and respect for the site, the architecture, and the client's vision, while never sacrificing the potential for place making or the opportunity to create a design that pushes boundaries.

Paul Sangha believes that residential projects can be research opportunities for landscape experimentation. Once a week the firm associates gather for a weekly "crit." This open incubator for design ideas and theory is an opportunity to discuss their dreams and aspirations for the firm, such as developing more efficient on-site water retention systems, initiating a plan for improving foreshores on coastal property lines, and unraveling the values and demerits of filter cloth. The crits deepen the firm's practice not only by fostering innovation, but also engendering a supportive creative atmosphere among its members. This commitment and passion for landscape is evident in their designs, with each project building on the momentum of the last.

Every design is an authentic claim to the land that it inhabits, yet the experience of each garden is unique not just because of the particular features of the site, but also because every garden reflects a different client—their lifestyle, personality, habits, and idiosyncrasies. Each project is a fresh opportunity for design exploration. The designs evidence aspects of human diversity and the nature of creativity. Regardless of how personal they feel, each landscape rings timeless—resilient and resistant to culture's changing tastes.

Paul Sangha works synchronize the human and the landscape and articulate a vision that reflects the prowess of both. The gardens speak to a coexistence, one that is deep and raw and visceral. One that flashes in glimpses before your eyes.

EXPLORATIONS IN THE SPIRIT OF PLACE AND BEING

BY BYRON HAWES

Landscape architecture, as a métier, is one of the most complex, collaborative and wholly modern of all artistic pursuits. It is also one of the most misunderstood. Having said that, to experience the works of the firm Paul Sangha Landscape Architecture is to understand the marriage of myriad disciplines, between the natural and the fabricated, the palimpsest and the evolutionary, the aesthetic and the ideological.

Mr. Sangha founded the 12-person practice in Vancouver in 1999, after 10 years as a senior landscape architect and designer for Ron Rule Consultants Ltd. and three and a half years experience as a partner at Rule, Sangha and Associates Limited. He has been honoured as a gold medalist at the University of British Columbia's Landscape Architecture Program and is the driving force and principal donor of the Paul Sangha Limited Scholarship in Design Excellence at the University of British Columbia's School of Architecture and Landscape Architecture.

Sangha's work goes beyond the traditional 19th century Romanticism often inherent in Landscape Architecture, instead existing within a modern framework more congruent with the emergent ecological era and contemporary ideals of sustainability.

Contemporary landscape architecture, particularly as it is understood and practiced by Paul Sangha, is a complex and multi-faceted endeavour. While 'Architecture' in the public's eye is a specific term and carries with it a specific meaning embodied by structure, the concept of Landscape Architecture as envisioned by Paul Sangha, embodies horticulture, architecture, industrial design, curatorship, and interior design, as well as that "hybrid of architecture and landscape, culture and nature, and art and ecology" which Adnan Kaplan refers to in his written work.

Gilbert Laing Meason first coined the term landscape architecture in 'On The Landscape Architecture of the Great Painters of Italy' (London, 1828), defining it as a discipline that encompasses planning, management and design; as well as land preservation and restoration. Meason's definition clearly delineates the role of the landscape architect as one who shapes the space and terrain around a pre-existing architectural piece, or the ongoing development of an exterior space.

Poets, writers, and philosophers have expounded on the theme of gardens in their language, yet in Sangha's contemporary realization of landscape architecture those exterior botanical considerations are tempered by an adherence to a defining principle of Zen Buddhist garden design: that said exteriors link directly and inextricably, with the actual physical structure and its interiors. Essentially that the yin and yang of structural and surrounding design coalesce to form a sort of 'design tulpa'.

One of the most complex and confounding elements of landscape architecture is its dynamic nature. Perhaps more than any other aspect of art and design, landscape architecture is subject to nature and culture more or less equally, including the environment, climate, and ecology. Because of this, the landscape architect becomes a sort of painter, joining animate (plants, water, climate) and inanimate (surfaces, structures) on his palette, to ultimately provide the most poetic arrangement of the geographic, social, technical, creative, and aesthetic.

A truly extraordinary feature of the works of Sangha, when seen in a collection such as this, is his ability to stay true to the nature of the environs in which he's working. On a visit to Vancouver he took me to see a few of his works, and one was dumbstruck by the variation between styles, some of which are quite literally next door to one another. From the stark minimalism of a slate grey Arthur Erickson house to a more neoclassical residence, the experience suggests being worlds apart, and yet a common thread runs through the two, allowing their respective styles and permeating moods to dictate aesthetics and experience. From the former: all rectilinear geometry in striking slate, led gently through towards the old growth forest bursting out of a ravine in back; to the latter: subtly modernized with a patinated Corten steel and brushed aluminium water feature highlighting a massive sculptural installation cut out of a single piece of jade. Both feel as they ought to, perfectly in balance, and sublimely composed.

In general, the pursuit of design is a study in choices. One of Sangha's greatest strengths is his ability to address and distill those choices. To sort through the realities of vegetation, water, structures, soils and topography; alongside more practical concerns including art collections and client tastes; and arrive at something that looks as though it should have been there all the time, perfectly in situ.

Landscape architecture is subtle, delicate, and holistic. It's at its most comfortable when seen as a natural progression of something, be it a structure or a time period. Perhaps the most collaborative of art forms, it is interpretive rather than purely creative, beholden to the fact that the true progression of landscape is, and always will be, left to the mercy of nature herself.

That interplay between art and space, that conflation of reality and the ideal, manifested in the realm between our senses, imaginations, aesthetics and experiences, is the basis for what Krystallia Kamvasinou referred to as "territory with hidden poetics," and the works of Sangha are rife with them. You can't simply stroll through one of Sangha's gardens, they cloak you, whispering alongside as you descend into the realm of the experiential.

In Sangha's version of landscape architecture, all aspects are given equal attention. While the gardens emerge as a clear way to revitalize one's surroundings through the presence of inviting spaces, they are just one ingredient in the overall experience. They are, however, unique in the sense that they require specifically predictive planning, as their natural imperative of growth is an open-ended sequence of transformative action.

As cohesive units, each Sangha project is emblematic of his 'walls out' approach, where he quite literally begins at the exterior walls of a primary structure (typically a residence), and crafts a cohesive experience that is clear, clean, and infinitely inviting. Sangha ably plays with spatial possibilities using landscaping and additions (including water features, gazebos, ponds, artisan-crafted paths and railings, a perfectly situated piece of sculpture), as well as playing with axial relationships, to create spaces that lure one in, placing them not in a location, but in a context.

Contemporary thinking suggests that landscape and objects have switched roles. That while once sculptures or secondary structures were placed to rivet the eye within a landscape, now landscape is a farm for highlighting those pieces in the most interesting way (Marc Treib, 2010). Yet in Sangha's approach they are two sides of the same coin, nouns and verbs, equally instrumental in the penning of an intensely harmonious stanza.

Sangha's works delight in their environment, taking full advantage of the climate and luminescent qualities of the Pacific Northwest. His juxtaposition of the muted palettes of locally-favoured building material and vibrant hues of the dizzying array of local vegetation is seamlessly emblematic of place.

Mr. Sangha himself has often spoken of his reductionist philosophies, saying that he endeavours to achieve a sort of zen stealth, arriving at that collocation of the genetic, dynamic and functional between the components of each part of the land surface in as few moves as possible. Advocating sustainability, re-use, and re-purposing, his aesthetic, ideological and philosophical goals are not only to be lauded, they are to be aspired to. However, as is often the case with true art, one's most vivid feelings are experiential. As such, perhaps the greatest compliment I can bestow upon Mr. Sangha is that, now that I have experienced the nourishing, introspective, virtually spectral majesty of his work, I consider it a great tragedy that I don't have access to one of his sublime respites for myself.

A Short Conversation Between the Author and the Subject

Byron Hawes: *How did you get into landscape architecture as a métier?*

Paul Sangha: Design is a passion and an addiction; it consumes me, rewards me, and challenges me. I enjoy every aspect of design, but the key is in the purity of approach and the magnificence of well-executed details. Landscape architecture is my métier, but within it is the reality that I can be a gardener, an architect, an interior designer, and a sculptor. They coexist in this profession, and as such, it is about the sculpting of spaces we occupy, both in this dimension and one which occupies time and seasons.

BH: *You and your firm's style clearly exhibits a strong kinship with traditional architecture, an almost symbiotic relationship between traditional architecture and landscape architecture. Could you elaborate on the interconnectedness of the two disciplines?*

PS: If the word "traditional" is about a renaissance attitude of artist, designer, and craftsman, then yes, my firm embraces "traditional" architecture. However, what I find today is that so much of what we do has been slotted into compartments. To be able to embrace an occupation like landscape architecture, you need to be able to build upon an understanding of "traditional" architecture, as well as light, nature, space, and human habitation so that meaningful experiences and spaces can be created.

BH: *On that note, there's a very common misnomer about landscape architecture wherein people oftentimes assume that it deals exclusively with plants and gardens, yet your work really focuses on the entire property from the house's walls out. Is this germane to the form, or more specific to your personal aesthetic?*

PS: I believe that my approach is unique within this profession. Early within my career, I realized that confining a thought process inhibits truly incredible designs. This process has become and is the signature of my firm. The objective is seamless design that is in tune with context, site, light, needs and architecture.

BH: *You've spoken at length on how lucky you feel to be working in Vancouver, given the breadth of vegetation and horticultural species that grow there. What are some of the primary advantages and disadvantages of working with Vancouver's climate ?*

PS: Vancouver is an incubator; it is a young, impressionable city with a thirst for all that is at the forefront of design, culture, and innovation. As a result, there is an openness in attitude and approach, allowing for possibilities that are only limited by one's imagination. This is what I feel most fortunate about—and most frightened about. I feel a tremendous responsibility to my clients, the community, and my profession to create work that will be timeless and as such, sustainable and adaptive to allow anyone to be able to experience them and come away moved, regardless of background—not only the first time, but every time they experience my work. Horticulture is the flesh of my projects and the wonderful opportunities that each climatic zone provides allow plants to express a project's regionality whilst transforming space, all within the context of a skeletal structure or static hard landscape.

BH: *To continue in that vein, Vancouver architecture has a very particular aesthetic, the 'grey sky architecture' style. How strongly does that influence you in the way that you design your work? And is it difficult, or liberating, to interact with such muted palettes?*

PS: "Grey sky architecture" absolutely requires a different colour palette and yes, I have chosen one that is muted. It stems from my desire to create space that is timeless, adaptive and open to one's own interpretation. I feel this palette facilitates a depth of experiences and interpretations. My work I hope is not literal; it is about the dance of summer light across this palette and the stark edge of the cold winter light with its low sun angles grazing surfaces, highlighting textures, and its contrast through shadow.

BH: *Your work evokes far more experiential, rather than simply aesthetic, reactions. How much of your process is centred around that draw, that usability, that invitation that your gardens present?*

PS: A key component of my work and design process is the exploration of the experiential. It is the experiences through contrast, the balance through fluid movement and the careful attention to detail by not snagging one's consciousness on flaws. It is about the enveloping calmness to take away the stress and struggles that embody one's journey through life. I hope that my gardens replenish one's soul, even though they are varied in style and scale.

BH: *Much has been made of your interest in sustainability. Yet in your projects you have made it clear that your concept of sustainability goes far beyond the traditional concept of sustainability of re-purposing materials into something very different. Could you explain it further?*

PS: My approach to sustainability is "less is more." I strive to be a reductionist; if I can convey an experience, an idea, a style through the least amount of intervention, I am finding purpose in my work and in the footprint it has. It is a lifelong goal to be able to express ideas with the fewest paintbrush strokes, and one I will never tire of. As I have grown with my work and even through the reflection allowed by this book, I have become more conscious about each brush stroke. I feel the health of this earth has to be inherent in any design process.

BH: *I've heard you referred to as the 'de la Quintinie of'. Mario Nievera's name has also come up. Are there landscape architects that you particularly admire, or whose work you feel strongly influenced by?*

PS: My inspiration comes from a respect for a way to live and experience life, and is heightened through being able to see the world through the eyes of others. My growth is being able to move outside my thought process to see the world through the eyes of sculptors like Joel Shapiro, the understanding of silence embodied by the teachings of J. Krishnamurti, the calmness that is a signature of Russell Page's gardens and the passion and violence of Picasso's paintings. My inspiration is ever changing and draws from everything that is around us. These varied perspectives allow me to distill and abstract both nature and experience in the work I do. Mario Nievera's work is indeed beautiful but I am more drawn to landscape architects like Roberto Burle Marx, Thomas Church, Dan Kiley, Fredrick Law Olmstead, Beatrix Farrand, Lawrence Halprin, and A.E. Bye.

THE **PROJECTS**

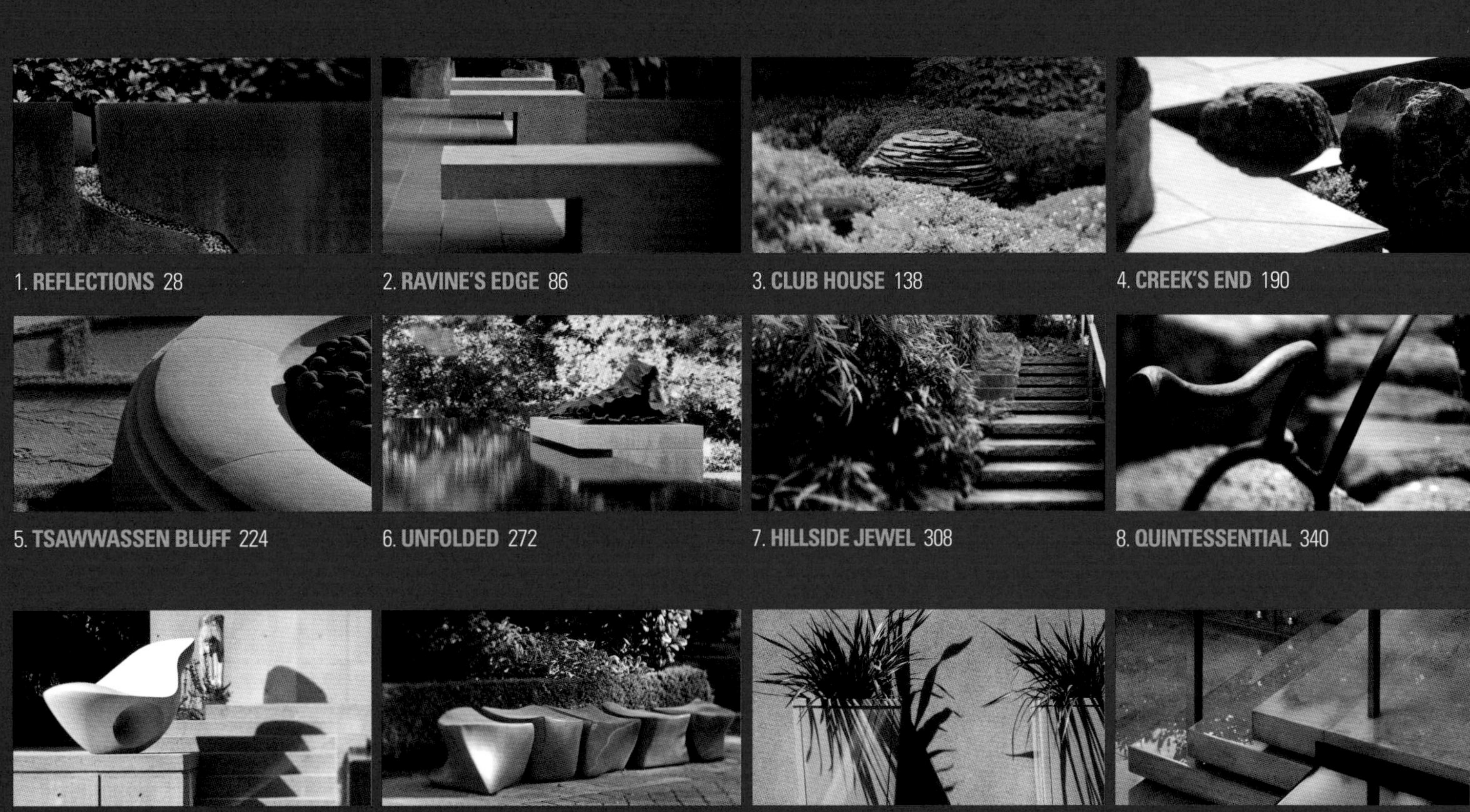

1. REFLECTIONS

White brachts of the Kousa Dogwood (*Cornus kousa*) hang delicately against the blue mountain backdrop, and perfectly shaped Leprechaun Ash (*Fraxinus pennsylvannica 'Johnson'*) stand in contrast to the breezy canopy beyond. Sculptures, which are placed throughout the terraced garden, keep the eye in stride with the foot: the rhythm of the walk feels harmonized with a rhythm of vision. The finely honed details in Reflections, such as the artist-commissioned wisteria stalk support system, focus the eye on the craftsmanship of the built environment while simultaneously engaging the natural topography of the background. The relationship between enclosure and expanse, the parti of the design, operates both to curate the visual experience and to define space. Ultimately, the design is an exercise in scale and balance—between the closeness of the garden and the majesty of the view.

Reflections, a garden designed for a client fond of entertaining, is indeed a leisurely, pleasurable place to be. A bocce court made from crushed oyster shells invites guests to play, a sunken fire pit allows them to relax, and a cedar-lined walkway through the untamed forest encourages them to discover. Though Reflections offers the perfect scene for any memorable occasion, it functions primarily as a restorative space, a stroll garden for the client—a place to walk the slowly paced paths, listen to the birds sing from their birdhouses, and watch the tide roll in. The garden's tranquility plays a role inside the house as well. From the master bedroom, the pool reflects the garden, collapsing the space of the landscape into a single frame and weaving the outside into the experience of the inside, the vastness of the view into the intimacy of the home.

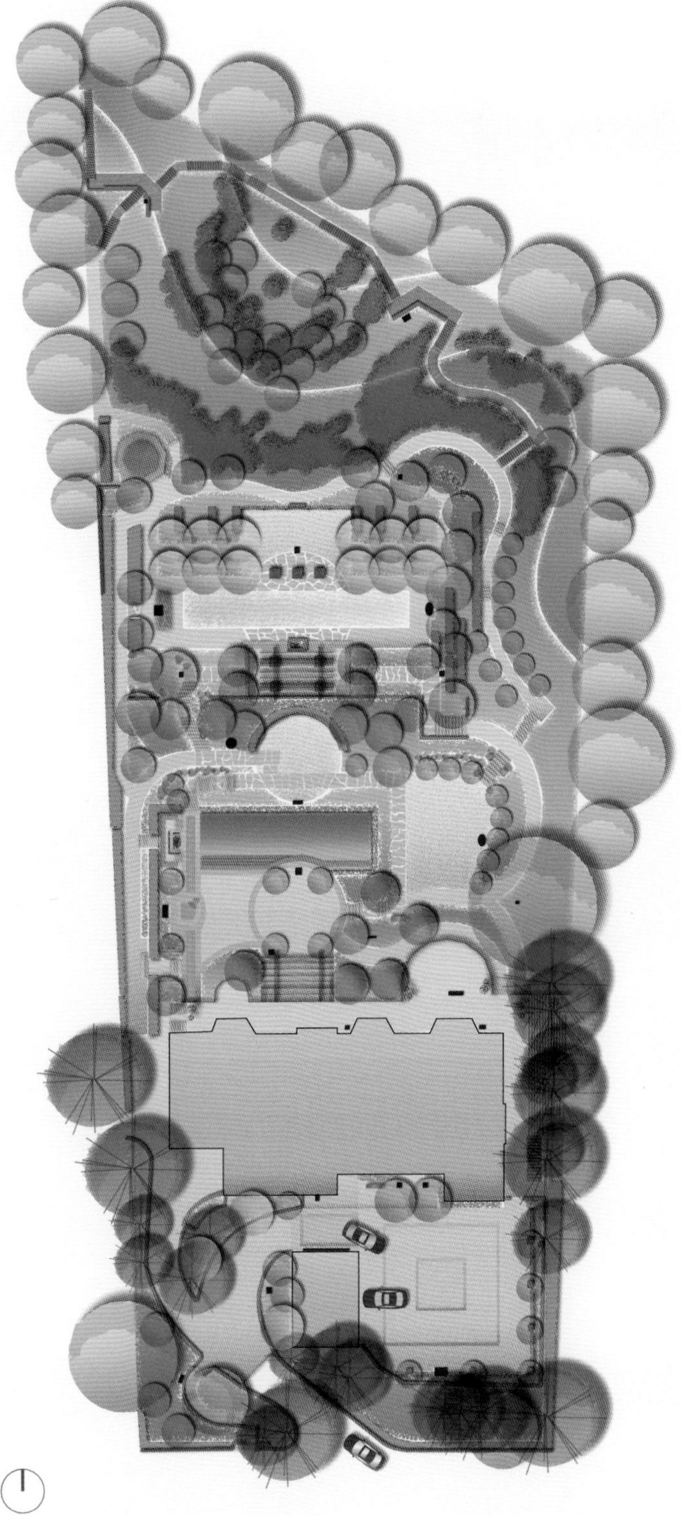

Left. An existing ramp provides a smooth transition between the upper terrace and pool levels.

Above. The garden's forms and textures balance the site's dramatic view.

Above. The terminus of an existing ramp connecting the upper patio and pool terrace is reconfigured from its previous location against the wall of the residence, to move through the garden.

Right. Glass railings replace existing carved wood panels along the ramp and upper patio, opening the space to the views beyond.

Left. A quartzite table sits on the pool terrace, directing the eye towards a focal sculpture and the expansive view. Leprechaun Ash (*Fraxinus pennsylvanica 'Johnson'*) frames the surrounding space.

Above Right. Views between interior and exterior spaces reinforce the axial relationships between home and garden.

Next Spread. The relationship between enclosure and expanse curates the visual experience and demarcates space.

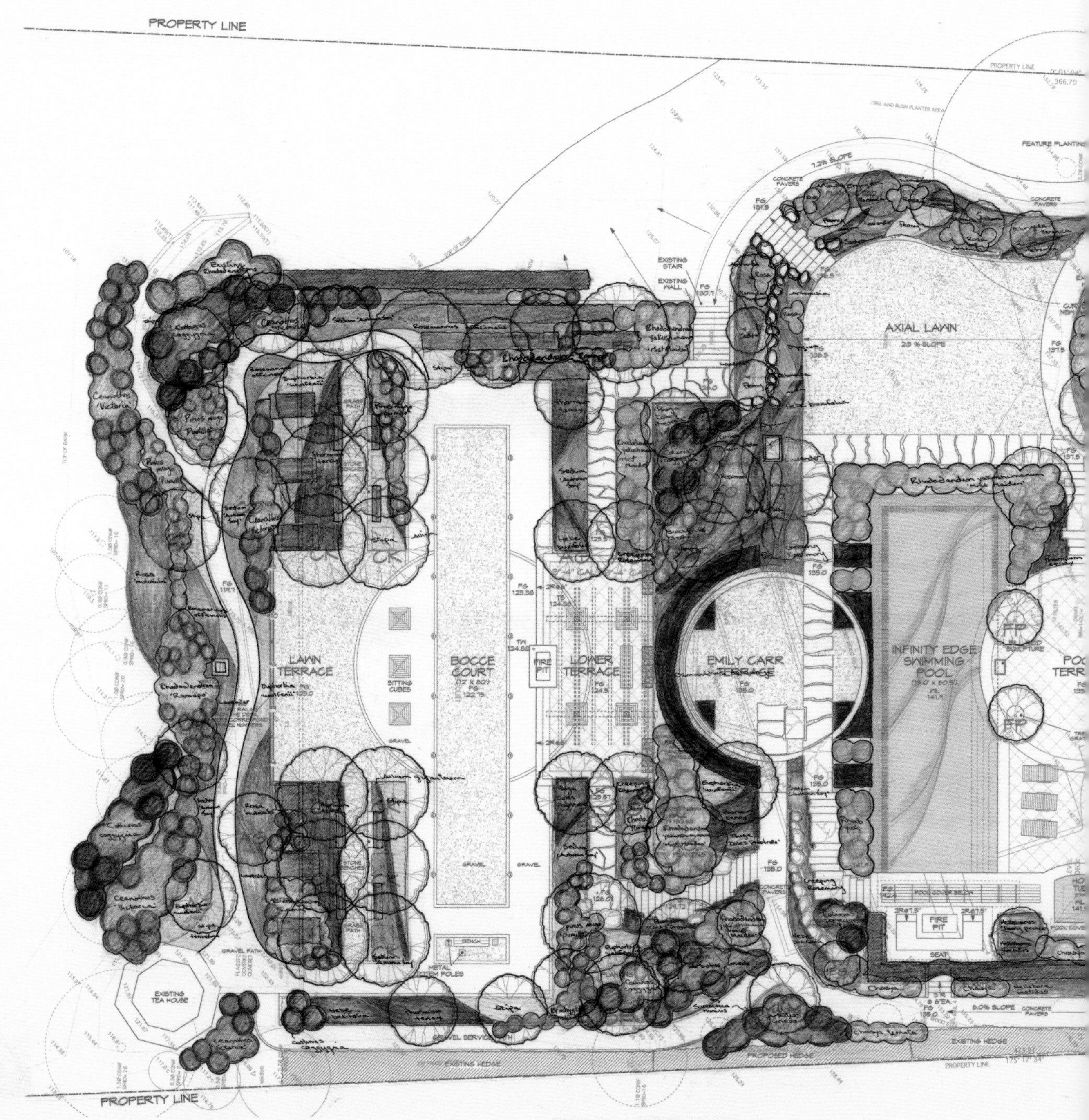

Above Right. Conceptual planting plan.

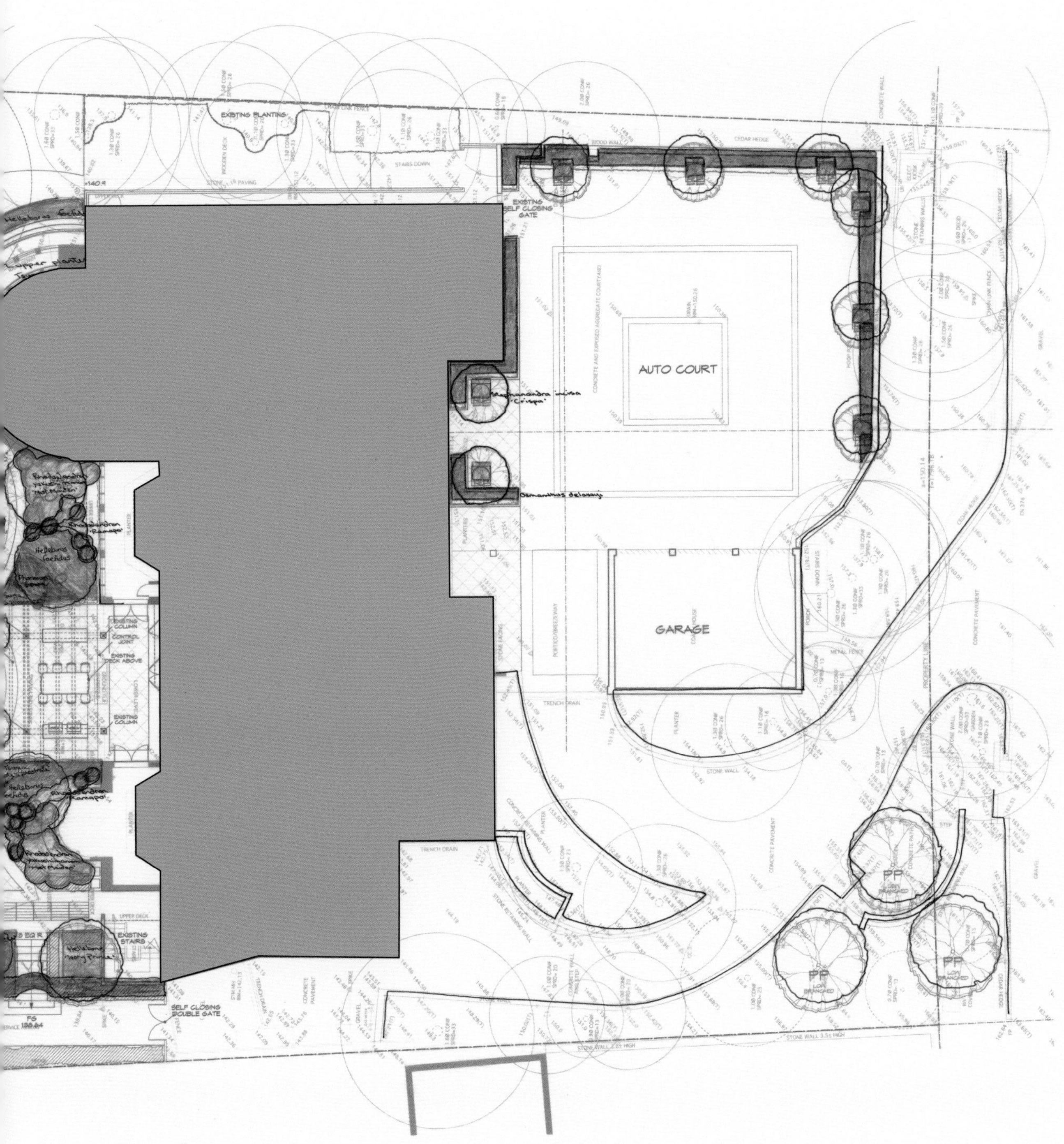
EXISTING PLANTINGS
EXISTING SELF CLOSING GATE
AUTO COURT
GARAGE
EXISTING COLUMN
EXISTING STAIRS
SELF CLOSING DOUBLE GATE
PP

Above. The surface of the pool reflects the changing sky, transforming the garden minute to minute.

Right. The pool weaves vastness and intimacy together, collapsing view, garden and home together within a defined frame.

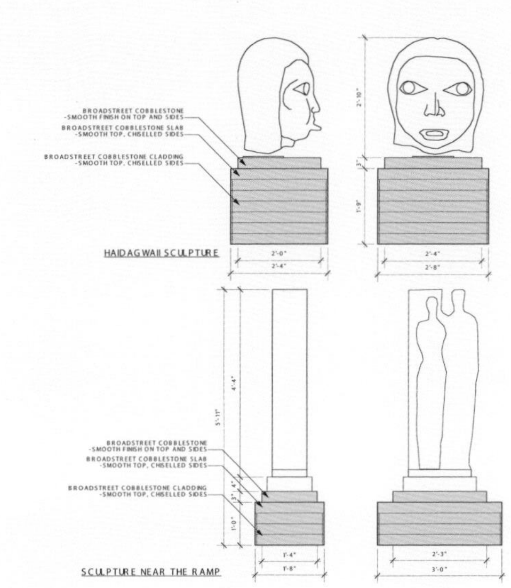

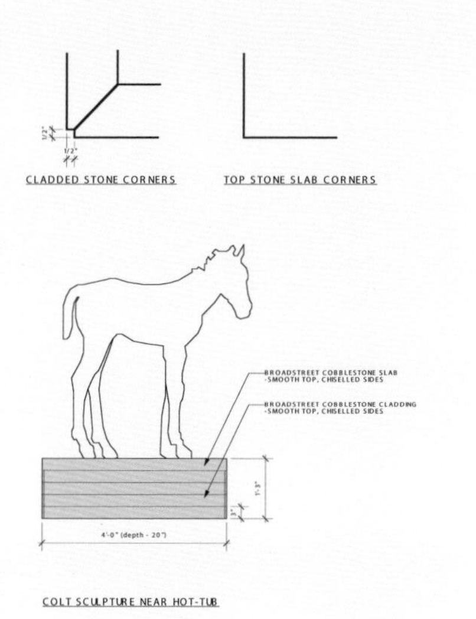

Left. A mirror to an everchanging landscape.

Above Right. At the north side of the pool, morning mist envelops the garden.

Far Right. 'Supernatural Eye' by Robert Davidson and uplit wisteria at the east side of the pool are a rhythmic backdrop for its mirrored surface.

Right. Sculpture base details.

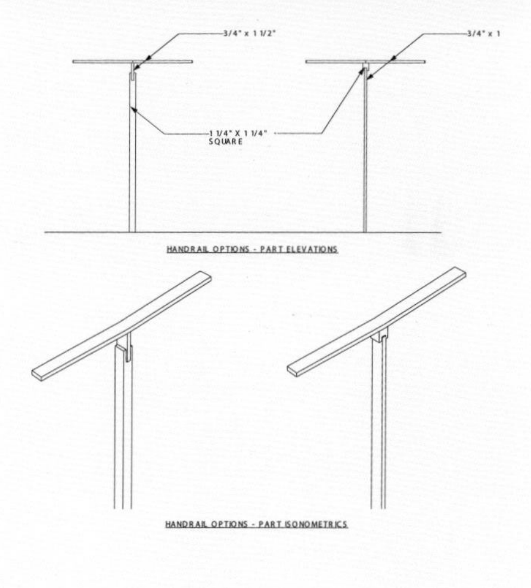

Above. Stainless steel grab rail detail.

Left. Early morning mist gives the garden a soft ambiance on cool mornings.

Next Spread. Acknowledging the play between garden and view, the landscape defines spaces for each to take precedent.

Previous Spread. With their jewel-like brachts drifting in the summer breeze, Wisteria (*Wisteria sinensis*) give soft definition to the space of the axial terrace.

Above. A shimmering wall of water offers a textural foil for the suspended sculpture on the north edge of the pool.

Right. A Corten wall sculpts topography while Sedums, Wisteria and "Sweet Box" (*Sarcococca*) softly define the boundaries of landscape rooms.

Previous Spread. Copper sheets of peeling Paperbark Maple (*Acer griseum*) contrast with the fine, geometric texture of Hebe.

Above. Red Masterwort *(Astrantia)* and Wisteria frame a view of an abstract stone sculpture.

Right. Persian Ironwood (*Parrotia persica*), Spurge (*Euphorbia*) and Smoke Bush (*Cotinus*) embrace a sculpture from the client's collection.

Left. A retaining wall provides a crisp canvas for Paperbark Maple *(Acer griseum)* and Rhododendron.

Right. A goalie playfully challenges players at the east end of the bocce court.

Above. Previously the location of a tennis court, the bocce terrace and pavilion offer an invitation to play and lounge.

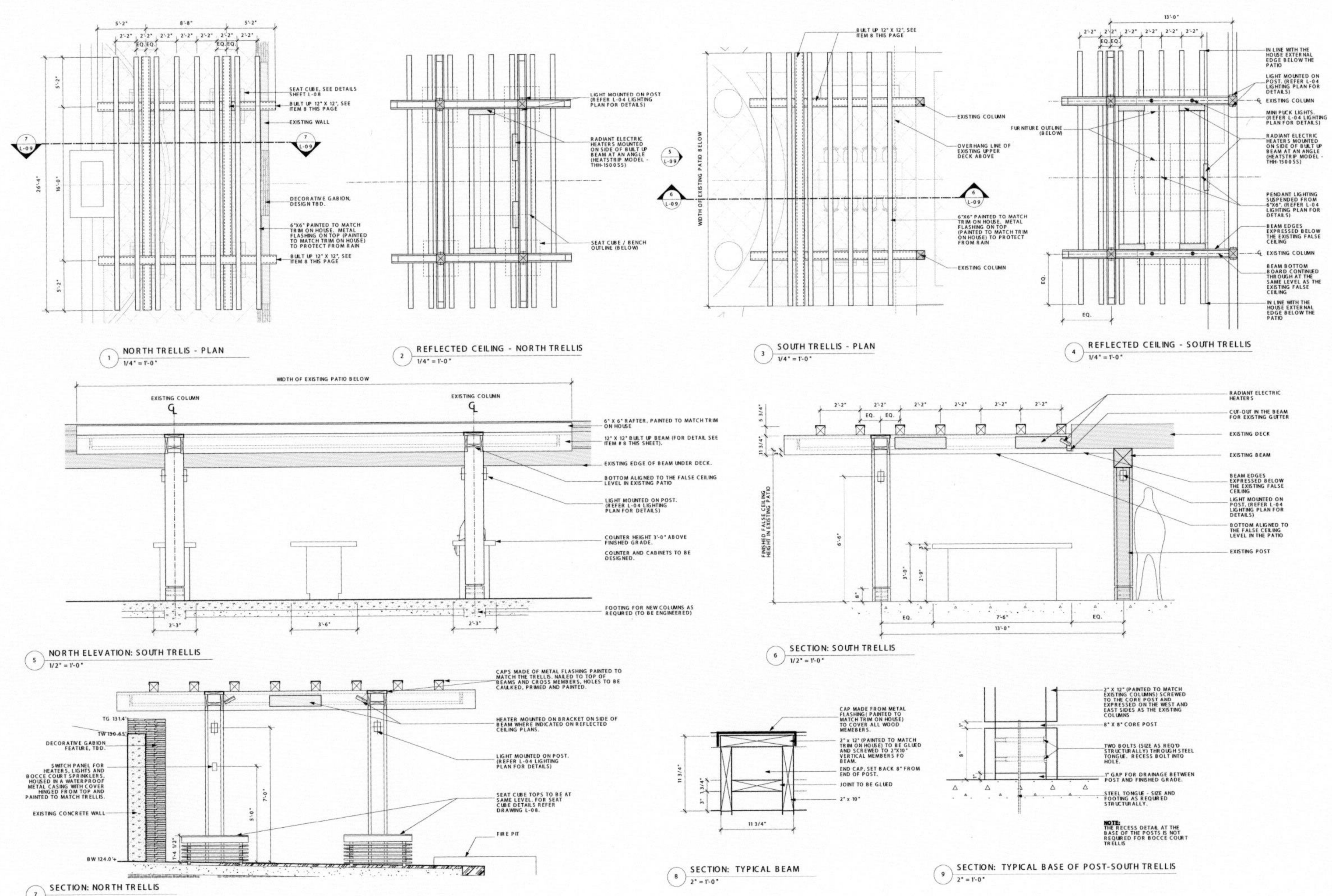

Above. Pavilion details.

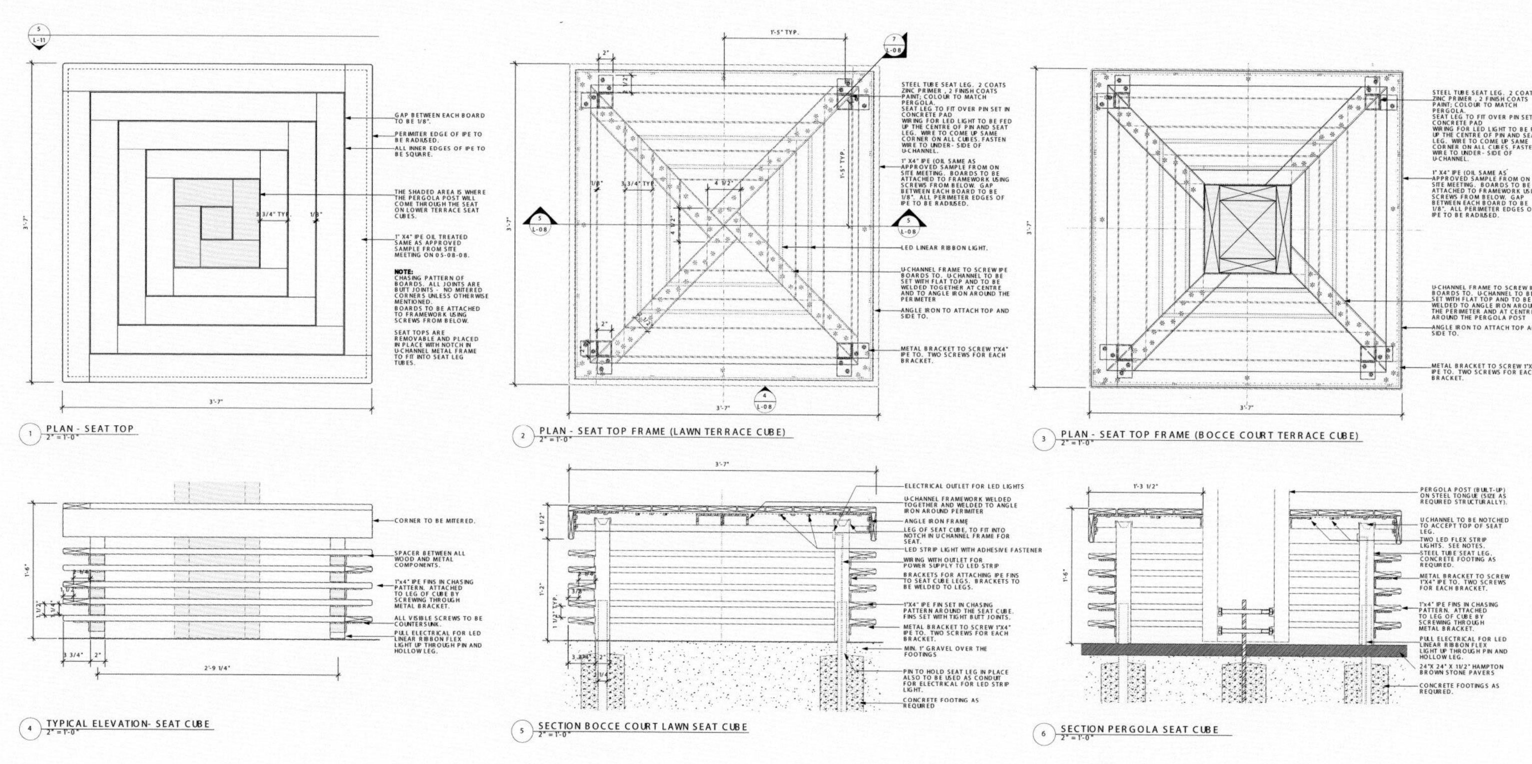

Above. Ipe seating cube details.

Above. Ipe seating cubes and recycled sculptural rails frame views from the bocce pavilion to the inlet and mountains beyond.

Above. Backdropped by a corten steel sculpture, the Bocce lounge provides an inviting vantage point for viewing.

Right. Ipe seating cube.

Left. A site-specific fractured Corten steel sculpture forms the north wall of the bocce pavilion.

Above. At the bocce court, crushed oyster shell and sandstone form a harmonious palette of texture and colour.

Left. With its watchful eye on the garden, a raven sculpture anchors the axis between the Bocce terrace and residence.

Left. Attention to detail expresses itself in the softly radiused edges of sandstone benches.

Right. 'Raven' terminates the axis of a pathway lined by inviting sandstone benches and Dogwood (*Cornus kousa*).

Next Spread. At the intersection of Sedum, Baby's Tears (*Soleirolia soleirolii*) and sandstone express scale and textural contrasts.

Above. Along the path connecting the axial terrace and bocce court, leaves of Aztec Pearl Mexican Mock Orange (*Choisya ternata 'Aztec Pearl'*) contrast with decorative carved wood railings.

Above Right. Axial views visually connect the garden's rooms while indirect paths allow participation in the stroll.

Above Left. With their sandstone-like colour, creamy blooms of Hebe aesthetically link the hardscape and planting.

Above. At the southwest corner of the bocce court Spurge (*Euphorbia*) and Persian Ironwood (*Parrotia persica*) envelop a sculpture from the client's collection.

Above. Embankment plantings of Sumac (*Rhus*) and Smoke Bush (*Cotinus*) create spectacular fall interest.

Right. Crisp lines of cedar rails and stainless steel airplane wire contrast the filigree of Sumac (*Rhus*) branches in the embankment walk.

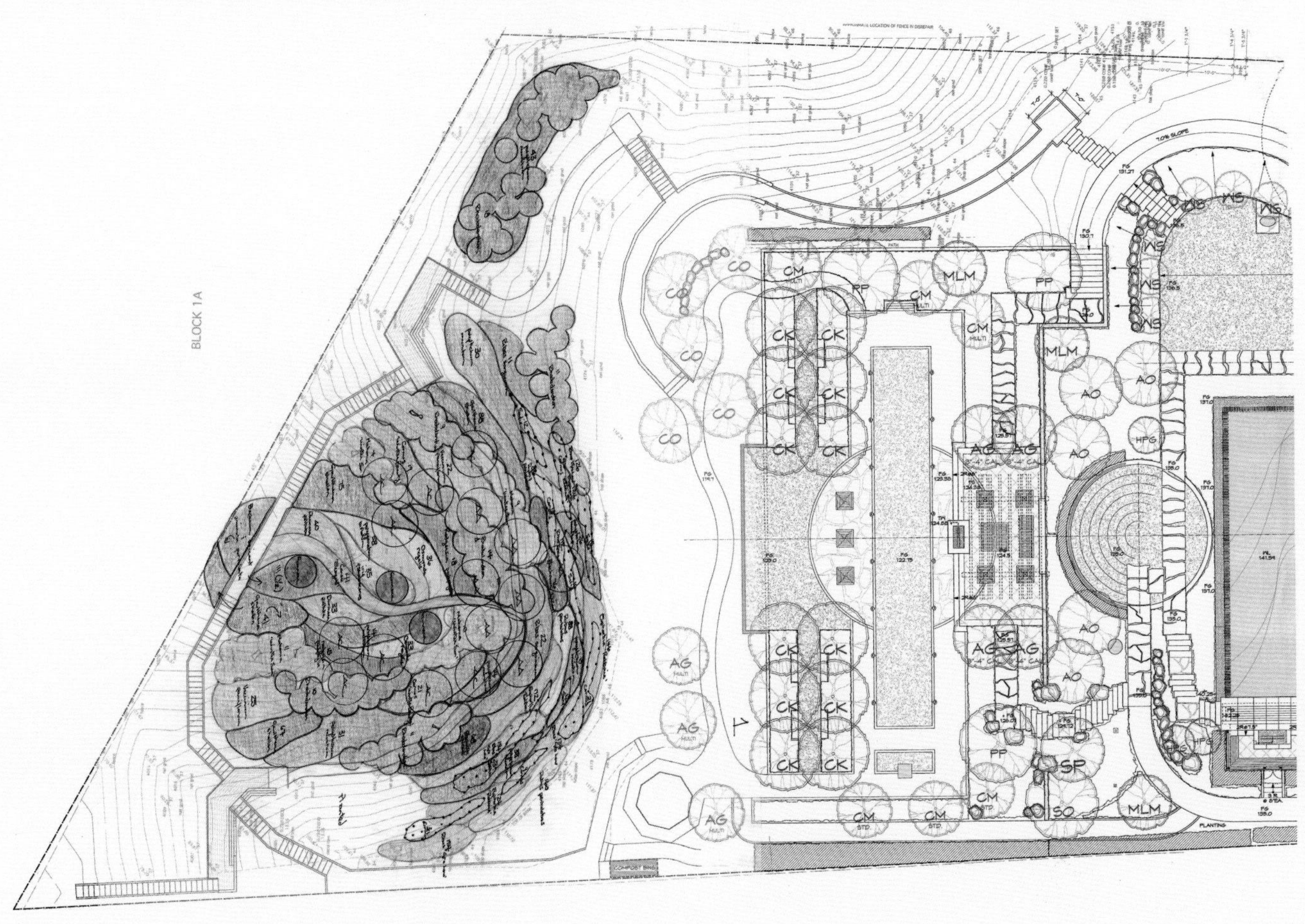

Left. A floating staircase and walkway reclaims access to the once neglected embankment.

Above. Embankment planting plan.

Above. Birdhouses punctuate the embankment walk while transitions in the pathway hinge around sculptural elements.

Right. Fall colour and sculpture bring a sense of whimsy to the experience of the embankment.

DENVER

2. RAVINE'S EDGE

Covered in an abstraction of tree trunks, the entry gate foreshadows the dramatic scene to come. From the edge of an open, verdant lawn, a cantilevered viewing platform boldly stretches out over a ravine into the darkness of an old growth forest. The walk from the neat, open lawn to the wild, dense canopy is a meditation on transformation, and the end of the platform is a place to meet nature face to face. Framing the lawn, a path winds around the property's perimeter, connecting the viewing platform to a pavilion that offers a place to soak in the sounds of the wind rushing through the branches and view the spectacle of the flickering forest light. Cozy, sheltered from the elements, and with views out into the wilderness, the space feels just as much like a grotto as it does a pavilion.

Under an elegantly crafted open-faced trellis, the path leads to the auto court past a grove of Kousa Dogwood (*Cornus kousa*), Persian Ironwood (*Parrotia persica*), and interlocking hedges of Japanese Holly (*Ilex crenata*) and English Yew (*Taxus baccata*). A series of cascading pools with a dazzling green colour produced by biological filters lie on axis with the front door. Above the garage a rooftop garden planted with Mountain Hemlock (*Tsuga mertesiana*) gives privacy from the neighbors. From the driveway, the path reemerges among raised vegetable beds, raspberry bushes, and espaliered fig trees, which are situated conveniently just outside a side door to the kitchen. The path meanders down the side of the property through Mount Fuji Cherry Trees (*Prunus serrulata 'Mount Fuji'*) and various species of Rhododendron, finally reaching the pond and terrace on the far side of the house. Benches that in form resemble the open L-shape of the trellis dot the edge of the hardscape of the terrace, providing a foreground element to the view from the home.

Features throughout the garden—such as the benches, entryway pools, and trellis—all noticeably yet subtly evoke the home's architecture. Not only does the garden reinforce the design of the architecture, but the architecture also reinforces the design of the garden. And the dialogue between the two creates a compelling and rich site experience.

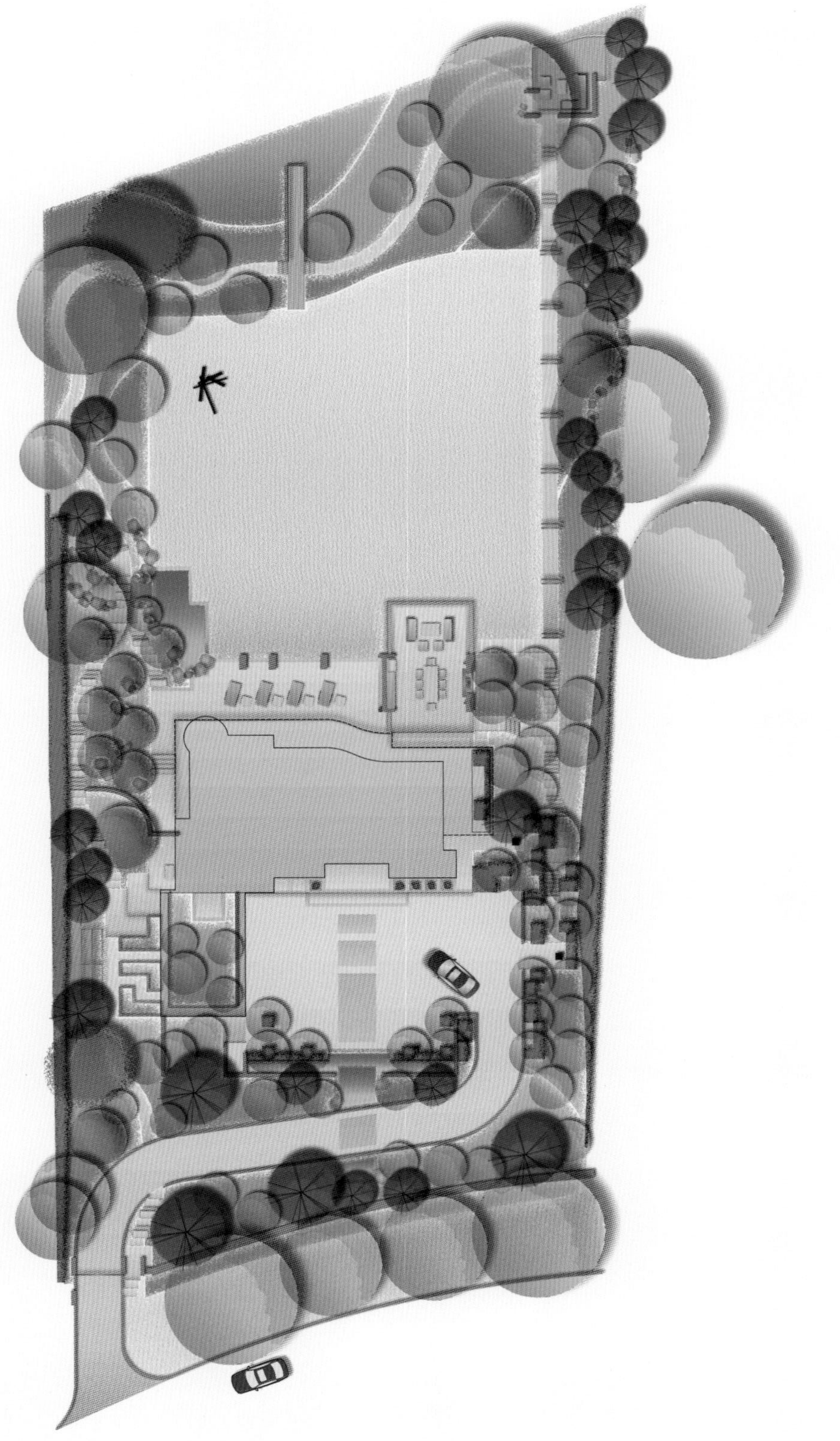

Left. The bespoke entry gate's vertical elements foreshadow the form of the second growth Douglas Fir trees that line the ravine beyond.

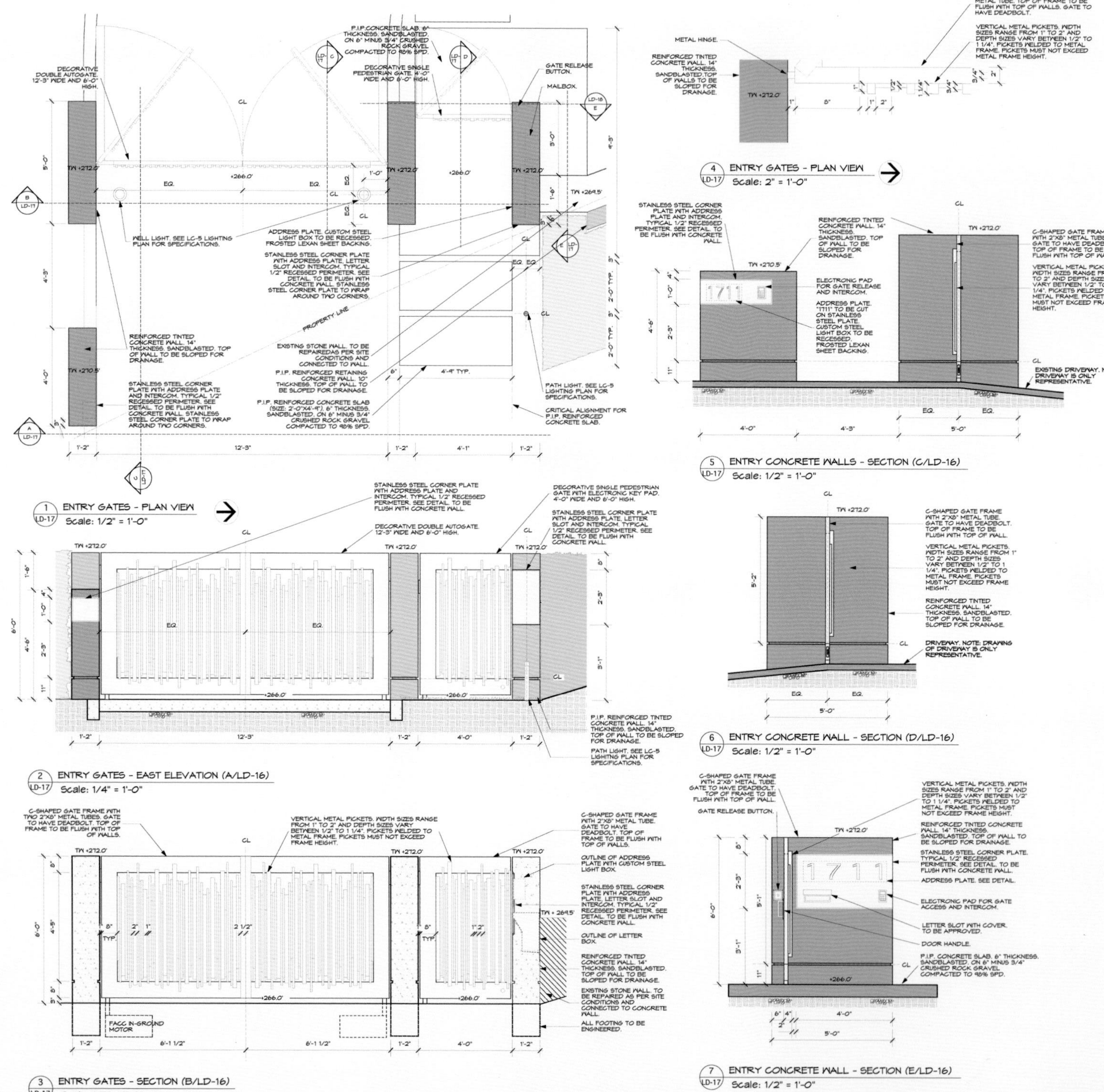
DECORATIVE DOUBLE AUTOGATE. 12'-3" WIDE AND 6'-0" HIGH.
P.I.P. CONCRETE SLAB. 6" THICKNESS. SANDBLASTED. ON 6" MINUS 3/4" CRUSHED ROCK GRAVEL COMPACTED TO 95% SPD.
DECORATIVE SINGLE PEDESTRIAN GATE. 4'-0" WIDE AND 6'-0" HIGH.
GATE RELEASE BUTTON.
MAILBOX.
WELL LIGHT. SEE LC-5 LIGHTING PLAN FOR SPECIFICATIONS.
ADDRESS PLATE. CUSTOM STEEL LIGHT BOX TO BE RECESSED. FROSTED LEXAN SHEET BACKING.
STAINLESS STEEL CORNER PLATE WITH ADDRESS PLATE, LETTER SLOT AND INTERCOM. TYPICAL 1/2" RECESSED PERIMETER. SEE DETAIL. TO BE FLUSH WITH CONCRETE WALL. STAINLESS STEEL CORNER PLATE TO WRAP AROUND TWO CORNERS.
PROPERTY LINE
REINFORCED TINTED CONCRETE WALL. 14" THICKNESS. SANDBLASTED. TOP OF WALL TO BE SLOPED FOR DRAINAGE.
EXISTING STONE WALL. TO BE REPAIRED AS PER SITE CONDITIONS AND CONNECTED TO WALL.
P.I.P. REINFORCED RETAINING CONCRETE WALL. 10" THICKNESS. TOP OF WALL TO BE SLOPED FOR DRAINAGE.
P.I.P. REINFORCED CONCRETE SLAB (SIZE: 2'-0"X4'-4"). 6" THICKNESS. SANDBLASTED. ON 6" MINUS 3/4" CRUSHED ROCK GRAVEL COMPACTED TO 95% SPD.
PATH LIGHT. SEE LC-5 LIGHTING PLAN FOR SPECIFICATIONS.
CRITICAL ALIGNMENT FOR P.I.P. REINFORCED CONCRETE SLAB.
1 LD-17 ENTRY GATES - PLAN VIEW
Scale: 1/2" = 1'-0"
METAL HINGE.
C-SHAPED GATE FRAME WITH 2"X8" METAL TUBE. TOP OF FRAME TO BE FLUSH WITH TOP OF WALLS. GATE TO HAVE DEADBOLT.
VERTICAL METAL PICKETS. WIDTH SIZES RANGE FROM 1" TO 2" AND DEPTH SIZES VARY BETWEEN 1/2" TO 1 1/4". PICKETS WELDED TO METAL FRAME. PICKETS MUST NOT EXCEED METAL FRAME HEIGHT.
4 LD-17 ENTRY GATES - PLAN VIEW
Scale: 2" = 1'-0"
ELECTRONIC PAD FOR GATE RELEASE AND INTERCOM.
ADDRESS PLATE. "1711" TO BE CUT ON STAINLESS STEEL PLATE. CUSTOM STEEL LIGHT BOX TO BE RECESSED. FROSTED LEXAN SHEET BACKING.
EXISTING DRIVEWAY. NOTE: DRIVEWAY IS ONLY REPRESENTATIVE.
5 LD-17 ENTRY CONCRETE WALLS - SECTION (C/LD-16)
Scale: 1/2" = 1'-0"
DRIVEWAY. NOTE: DRAWING OF DRIVEWAY IS ONLY REPRESENTATIVE.
6 LD-17 ENTRY CONCRETE WALL - SECTION (D/LD-16)
Scale: 1/2" = 1'-0"
DECORATIVE SINGLE PEDESTRIAN GATE WITH ELECTRONIC KEY PAD. 4'-0" WIDE AND 6'-0" HIGH.
P.I.P. REINFORCED TINTED CONCRETE WALL. 14" THICKNESS. SANDBLASTED. TOP OF WALL TO BE SLOPED FOR DRAINAGE.
2 LD-17 ENTRY GATES - EAST ELEVATION (A/LD-16)
Scale: 1/4" = 1'-0"
C-SHAPED GATE FRAME WITH TWO 2"X8" METAL TUBES. GATE TO HAVE DEADBOLT. TOP OF FRAME TO BE FLUSH WITH TOP OF WALLS.
OUTLINE OF ADDRESS PLATE WITH CUSTOM STEEL LIGHT BOX.
OUTLINE OF LETTER BOX.
EXISTING STONE WALL. TO BE REPAIRED AS PER SITE CONDITIONS AND CONNECTED TO CONCRETE WALL.
ALL FOOTING TO BE ENGINEERED.
FACC IN-GROUND MOTOR
3 LD-17 ENTRY GATES - SECTION (B/LD-16)
Scale: 1/2" = 1'-0"
GATE RELEASE BUTTON.
STAINLESS STEEL CORNER PLATE. TYPICAL 1/2" RECESSED PERIMETER. SEE DETAIL. TO BE FLUSH WITH CONCRETE WALL.
ADDRESS PLATE. SEE DETAIL.
ELECTRONIC PAD FOR GATE ACCESS AND INTERCOM.
LETTER SLOT WITH COVER. TO BE APPROVED.
DOOR HANDLE.
P.I.P. CONCRETE SLAB. 6" THICKNESS. SANDBLASTED. ON 6" MINUS 3/4" CRUSHED ROCK GRAVEL COMPACTED TO 95% SPD.
7 LD-17 ENTRY CONCRETE WALL - SECTION (E/LD-16)
Scale: 1/2" = 1'-0"

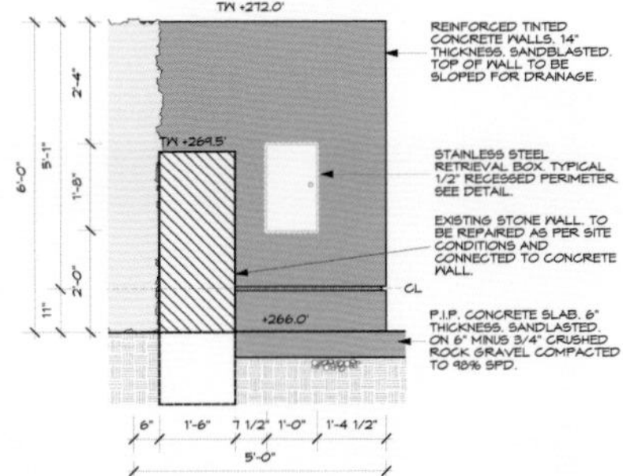

8 LD-17 ENTRY CONCRETE WALL - SECTION (F/LD-16)
Scale: 1/2" = 1'-0"

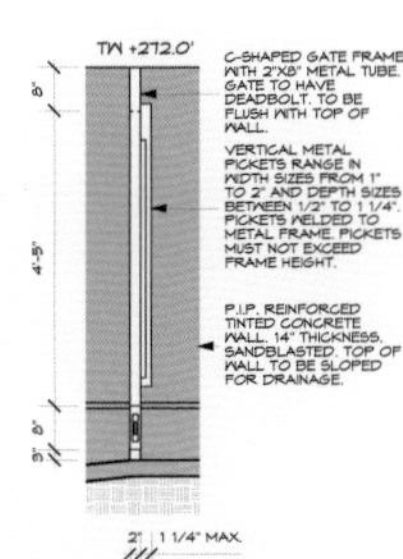

9 LD-17 ENTRY GATE - DETAIL
Scale: 3/4" = 1'-0"

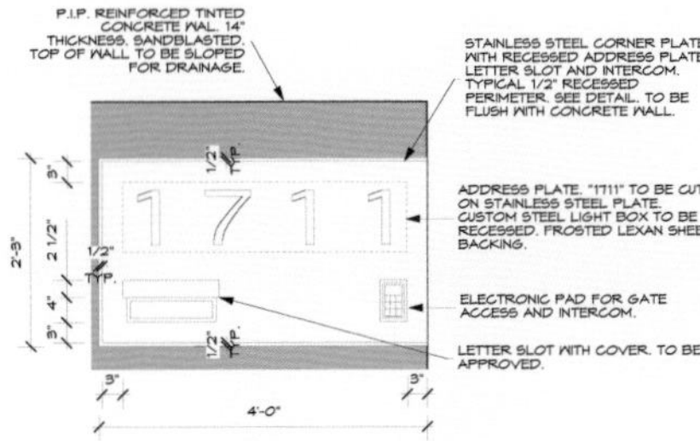

10 LD-17 PEDESTRIAN ADDRESS PLATE - DETAIL
Scale: 3/4" = 1'-0"

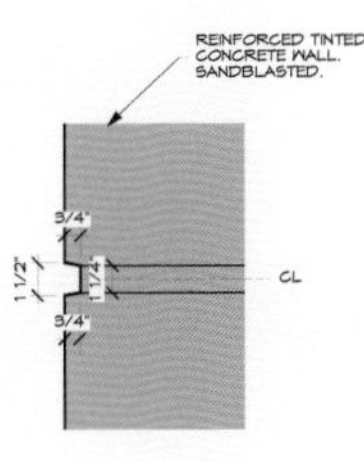

11 LD-17 TYPICAL REVEAL DETAIL
Scale: 2" = 1'-0"

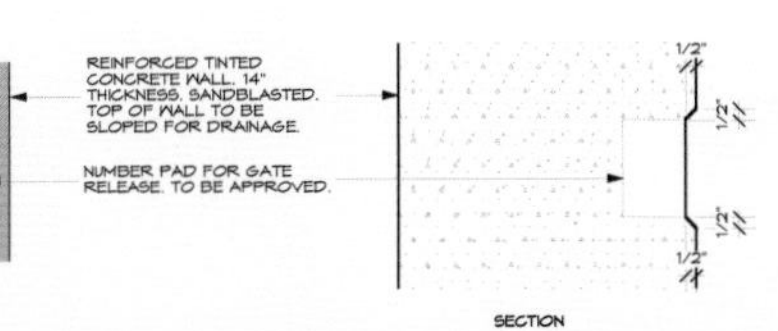

12 LD-17 TYPICAL 1/2" RECESSED PERIMETER - DETAIL
Scale: 2" = 1'-0"

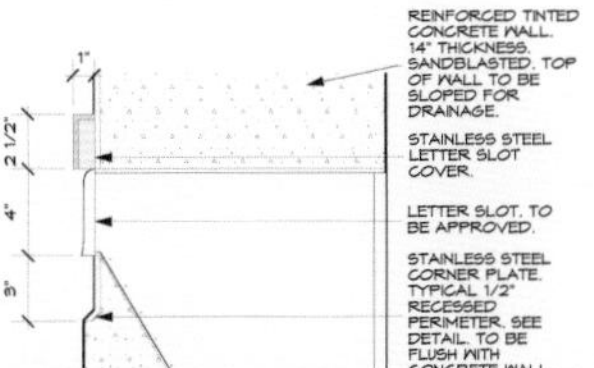

13 LD-17 LETTER SLOT & COVER - DETAIL
Scale: 2" = 1'-0"

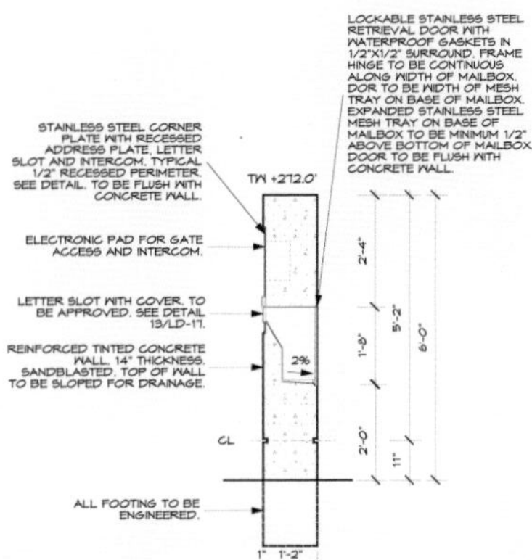

14 LD-17 PEDESTRIAN GATE - EAST ELEVATION
Scale: 1/2" = 1'-0"

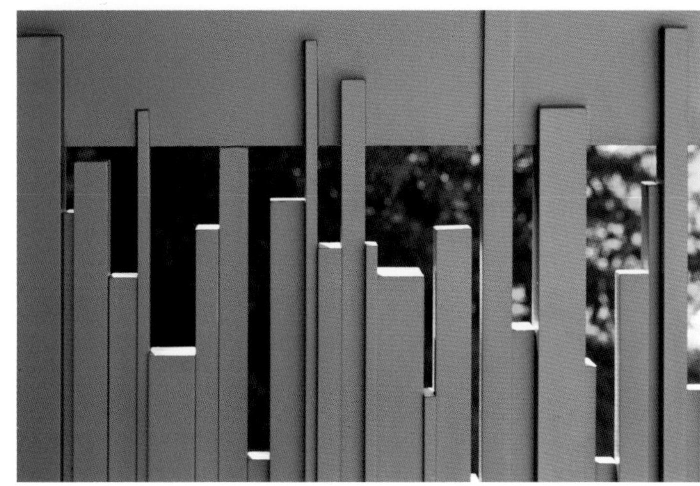

Above. Entry views.

Left. Entry details.

6 LD-16 AUTOCOURT ROCK FOUNTAIN - SECTION (C/LD-16)
Scale: 3/4" = 1'-0"

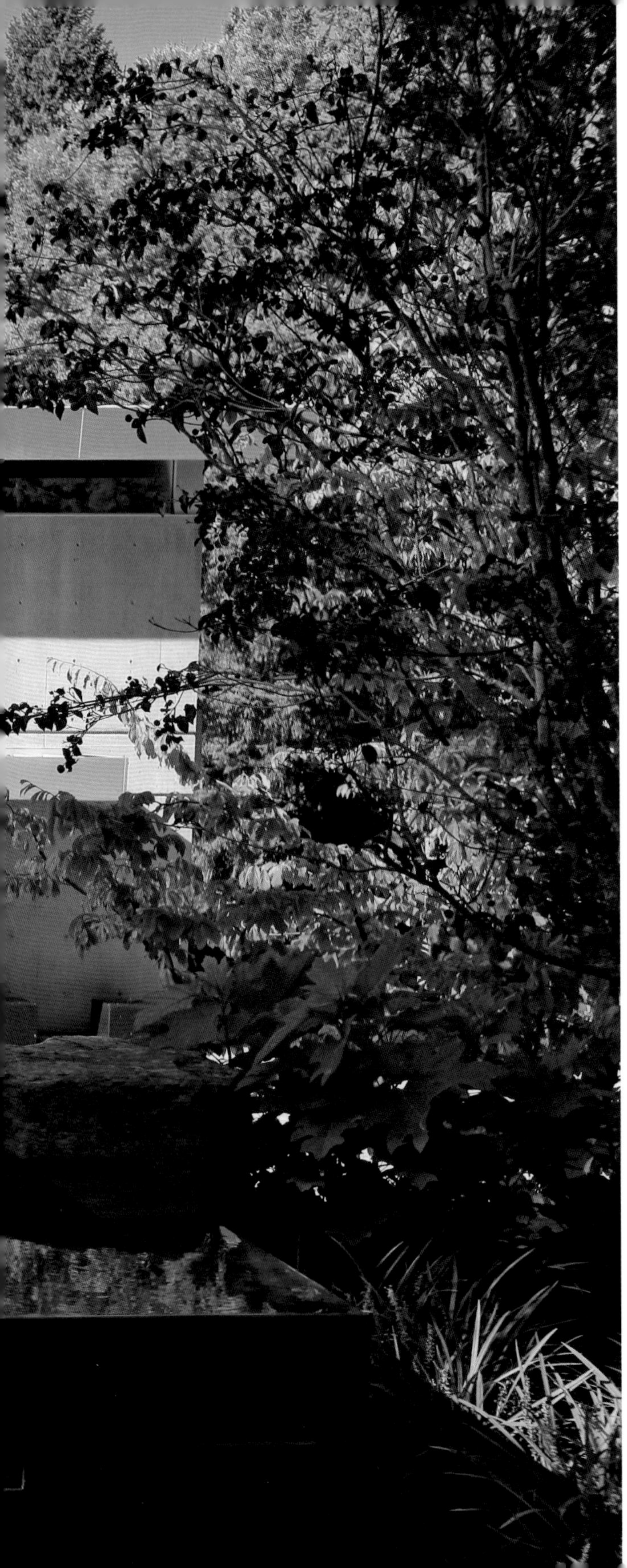

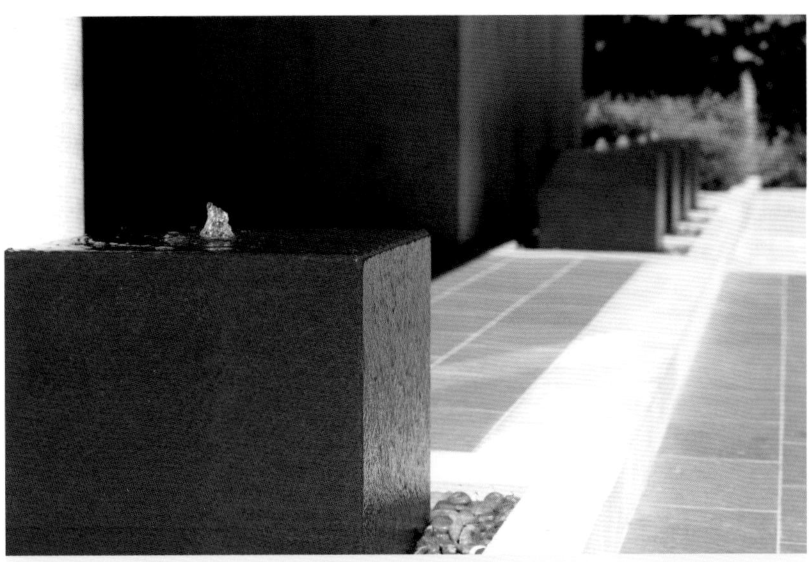

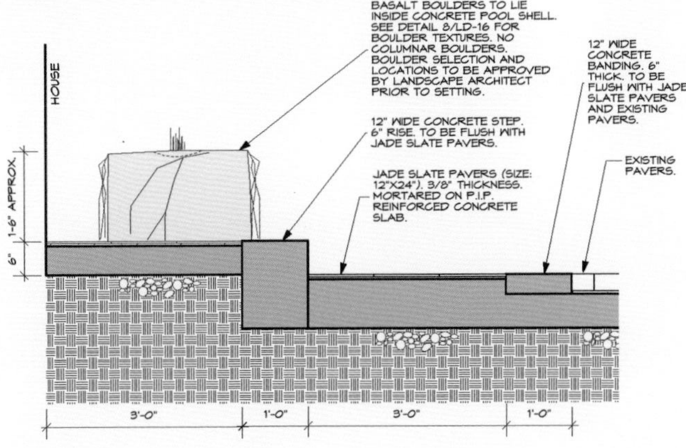

Left. An opening along the driveway frames a view to the residence across a reflecting pool.

Above. Detail of bubbling water cubes at the entry details.

Next Spread. In the autocourt, a bosque of Persian Ironwood (*Parrotia persica*) frames a shimmering slate water feature that sits on axis with the front door.

Left. Water dances over the autocourt's slate feature wall. The invisible edge reinforces the central axis connecting the autocourt and front entry.

Right. Water feature details.

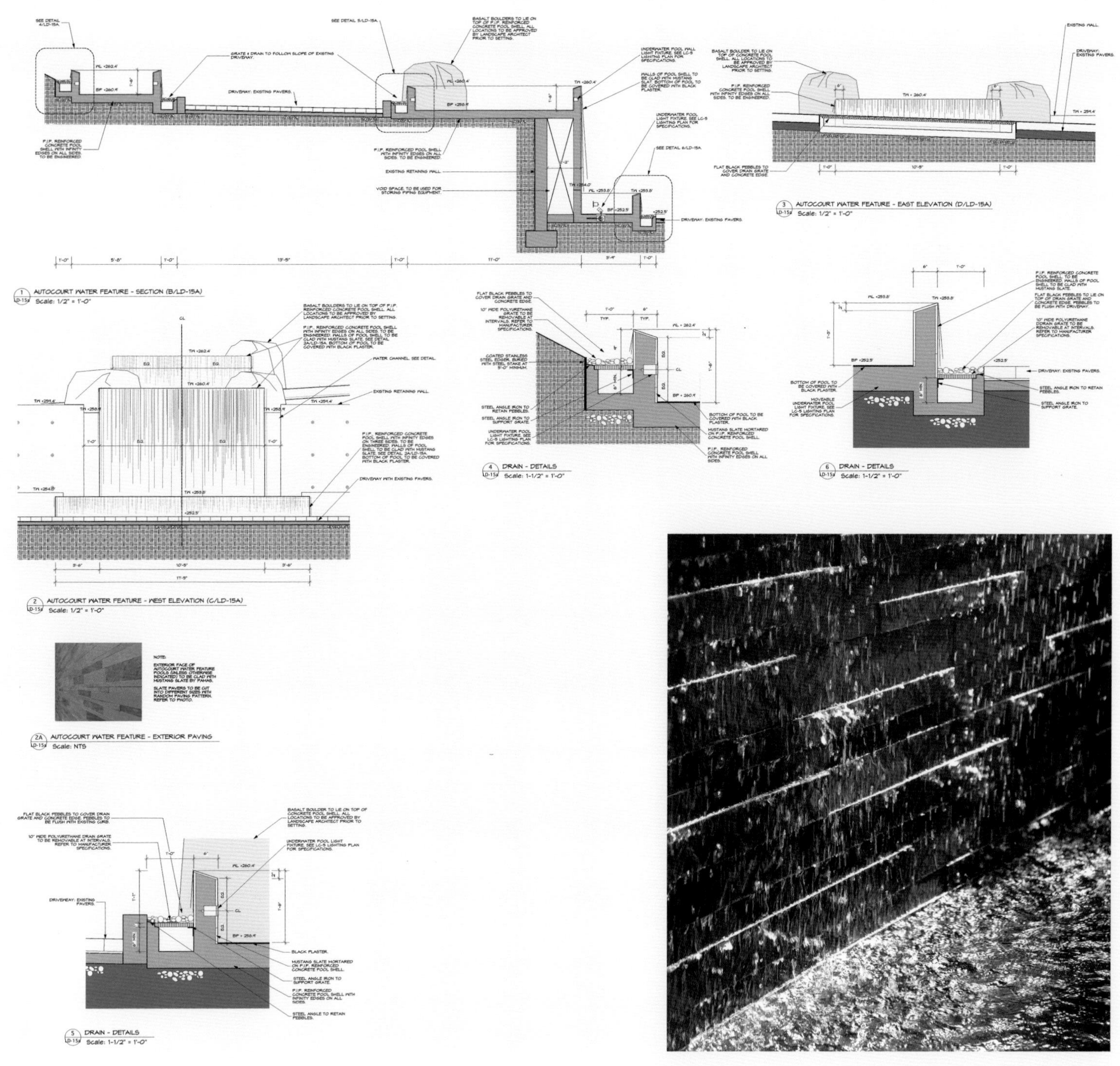
1 AUTOCOURT WATER FEATURE - SECTION (B/LD-15A)
Scale: 1/2" = 1'-0"
3 AUTOCOURT WATER FEATURE - EAST ELEVATION (D/LD-15A)
Scale: 1/2" = 1'-0"
2 AUTOCOURT WATER FEATURE - WEST ELEVATION (C/LD-15A)
Scale: 1/2" = 1'-0"
4 DRAIN - DETAILS
Scale: 1-1/2" = 1'-0"
6 DRAIN - DETAILS
Scale: 1-1/2" = 1'-0"
2A AUTOCOURT WATER FEATURE - EXTERIOR PAVING
Scale: NTS
5 DRAIN - DETAILS
Scale: 1-1/2" = 1'-0"

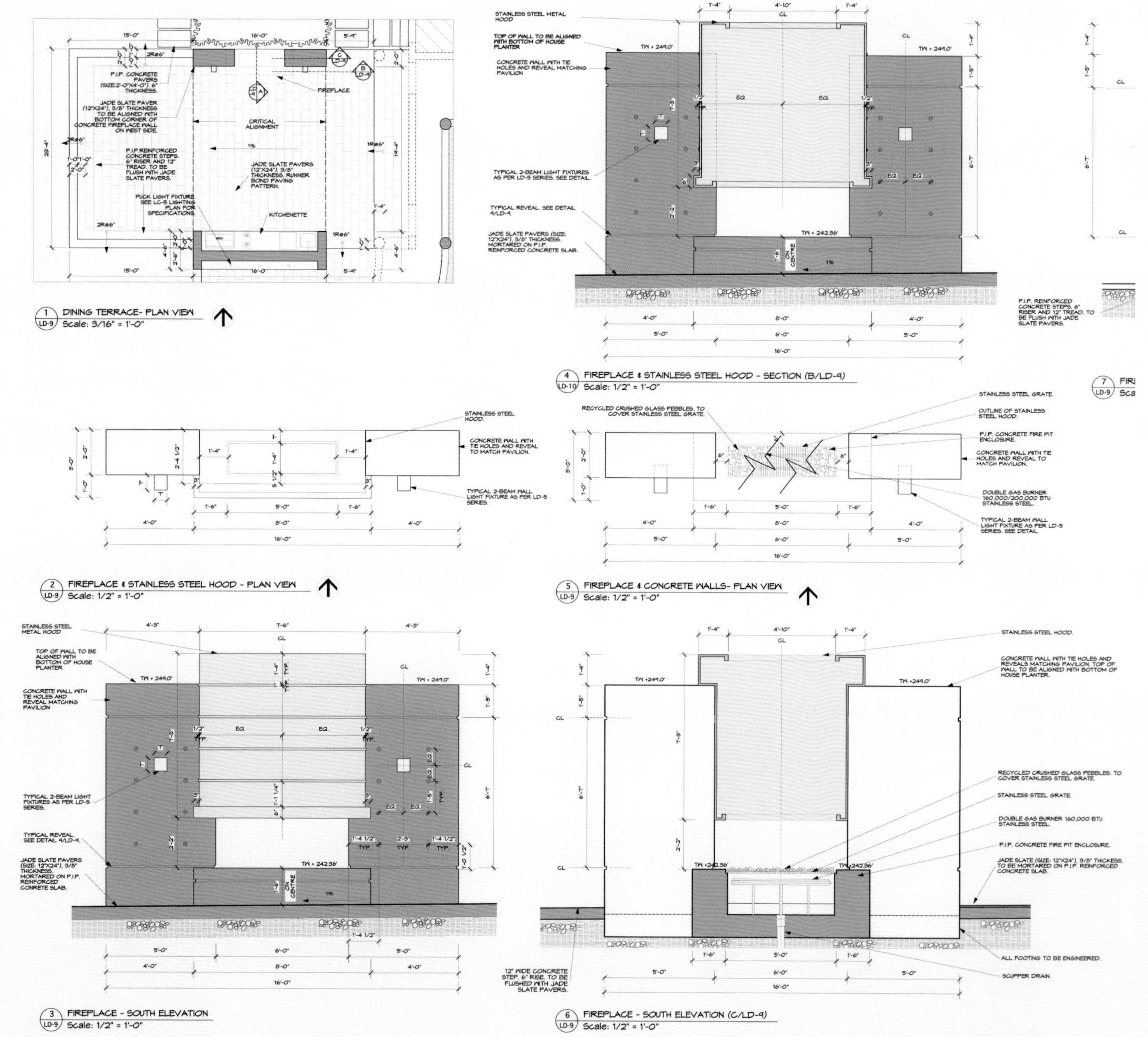
1 LD-9 DINING TERRACE- PLAN VIEW
Scale: 3/16" = 1'-0"
P.I.P. CONCRETE PAVERS (SIZE:2'-0"X4'-0"), 6" THICKNESS.
JADE SLATE PAVER (12"X24"), 3/8" THICKNESS TO BE ALIGNED WITH BOTTOM CORNER OF CONCRETE FIREPLACE WALL ON WEST SIDE.
P.I.P. REINFORCED CONCRETE STEPS. 6" RISER AND 12" TREAD. TO BE FLUSH WITH JADE SLATE PAVERS.
PUCK LIGHT FIXTURE. SEE LC-5 LIGHTING PLAN FOR SPECIFICATIONS.
FIREPLACE
CRITICAL ALIGNMENT
JADE SLATE PAVERS (12"X24"), 3/8" THICKNESS. RUNNER BOND PAVING PATTERN.
KITCHENETTE
4 LD-10 FIREPLACE & STAINLESS STEEL HOOD - SECTION (B/LD-9)
Scale: 1/2" = 1'-0"
STAINLESS STEEL METAL HOOD
TOP OF WALL TO BE ALIGNED WITH BOTTOM OF HOUSE PLANTER
CONCRETE WALL WITH TIE HOLES AND REVEAL MATCHING PAVILION
TYPICAL 2-BEAM LIGHT FIXTURES AS PER LD-5 SERIES. SEE DETAIL.
TYPICAL REVEAL. SEE DETAIL 4/LD-9.
JADE SLATE PAVERS (SIZE: 12"X24"), 3/8" THICKNESS. MORTARED ON P.I.P. REINFORCED CONCRETE SLAB.
P.I.P. REINFORCED CONCRETE STEPS. 6" RISER AND 12" TREAD. TO BE FLUSH WITH JADE SLATE PAVERS.
2 LD-9 FIREPLACE & STAINLESS STEEL HOOD - PLAN VIEW
Scale: 1/2" = 1'-0"
STAINLESS STEEL HOOD.
CONCRETE WALL WITH TIE HOLES AND REVEAL TO MATCH PAVILION.
TYPICAL 2-BEAM WALL LIGHT FIXTURE AS PER LD-5 SERIES.
5 LD-9 FIREPLACE & CONCRETE WALLS- PLAN VIEW
Scale: 1/2" = 1'-0"
RECYCLED CRUSHED GLASS PEBBLES. TO COVER STAINLESS STEEL GRATE.
STAINLESS STEEL GRATE.
OUTLINE OF STAINLESS STEEL HOOD.
P.I.P. CONCRETE FIRE PIT ENCLOSURE.
CONCRETE WALL WITH TIE HOLES AND REVEAL TO MATCH PAVILION.
DOUBLE GAS BURNER 160,000/200,000 BTU STAINLESS STEEL.
TYPICAL 2-BEAM WALL LIGHT FIXTURE AS PER LD-5 SERIES. SEE DETAIL.
3 LD-9 FIREPLACE - SOUTH ELEVATION
Scale: 1/2" = 1'-0"
STAINLESS STEEL METAL HOOD
TOP OF WALL TO BE ALIGNED WITH BOTTOM OF HOUSE PLANTER
CONCRETE WALL WITH TIE HOLES AND REVEAL MATCHING PAVILION
TYPICAL 2-BEAM LIGHT FIXTURES AS PER LD-5 SERIES.
TYPICAL REVEAL. SEE DETAIL 4/LD-9.
JADE SLATE PAVERS (SIZE: 12"X24"), 3/8" THICKNESS. MORTARED ON P.I.P. REINFORCED CONRETE SLAB.
6 LD-9 FIREPLACE - SOUTH ELEVATION (C/LD-9)
Scale: 1/2" = 1'-0"
STAINLESS STEEL HOOD.
CONCRETE WALL WITH TIE HOLES AND REVEALS MATCHING PAVILION. TOP OF WALL TO BE ALIGNED WITH BOTTOM OF HOUSE PLANTER.
RECYCLED CRUSHED GLASS PEBBLES. TO COVER STAINLESS STEEL GRATE.
STAINLESS STEEL GRATE.
DOUBLE GAS BURNER 160,000 BTU STAINLESS STEEL.
P.I.P. CONCRETE FIRE PIT ENCLOSURE.
JADE SLATE (SIZE: 12"X24"), 3/8" THICKESS. TO BE MORTARED ON P.I.P. REINFORCED CONCRETE SLAB.
ALL FOOTING TO BE ENGINEERED.
SCUPPER DRAIN.
12" WIDE CONCRETE STEP. 6" RISE. TO BE FLUSHED WITH JADE SLATE PAVERS.

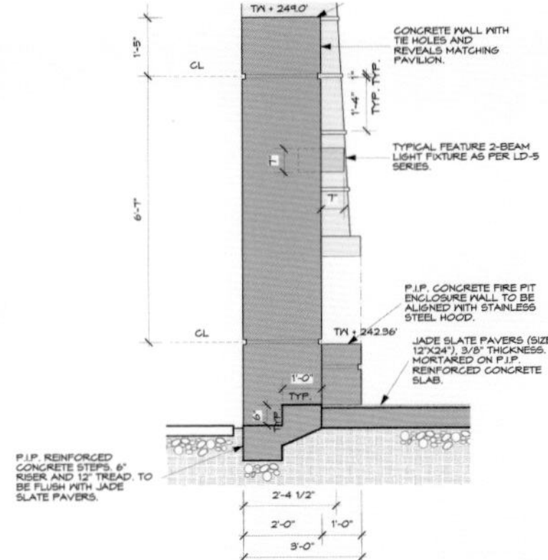

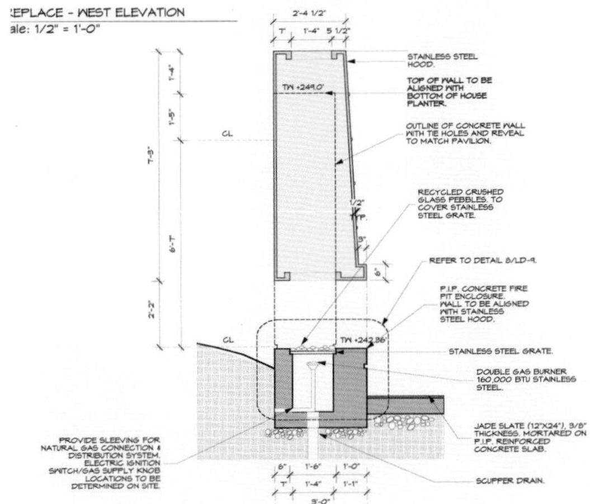

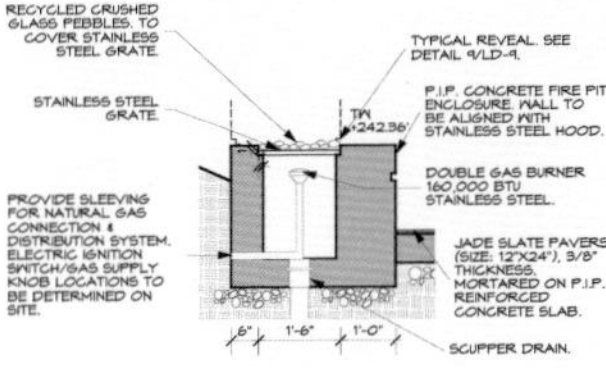

Above. Fireplace details.

Next Spread. At the pool terrace, concrete seating forms visually connect to the outdoor kitchen articulating the intersection of the terrace and lawn.

Above. Rolling lawn provides ample space in which to play.

Right. Supported on one side only, the arbor embraces the lawn and walkway while framing the axial entry to the ravine pavilion.

Left. Perched at the ravine's edge, the pavilion is a portal to the native west coast landscape.

Above. The cantilevered roof of the ravine pavilion provides a strong and sensitive counterpoint to the vertical forms of the surrounding trees.

Right. The pavilion's roof and Ipe floor frames the ravine for the contemplative interior space.

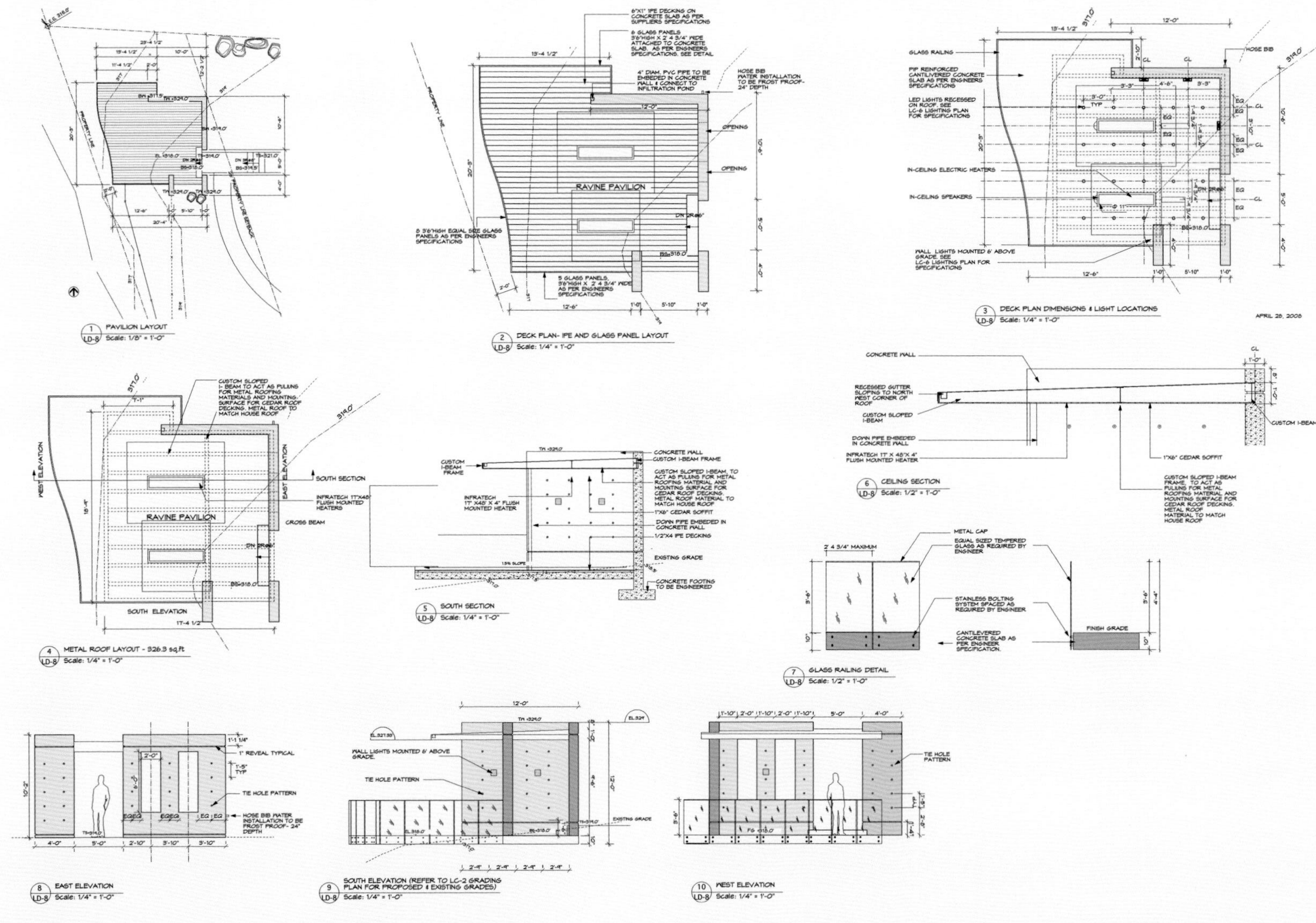

Above. Pavilion details.

Above. A solid concrete wall directs views to the southwest.

Left. In the ravine, Maidenhair Fern (*Adiantum pedatum*) cascades over a pathway of crushed basalt.

Right. Contrasting textures and colours provide lush visual interest throughout the year.

Left. An Ipe catwalk cantilevered over the ravine allows for a unique experience of the coniferous forest canopy.

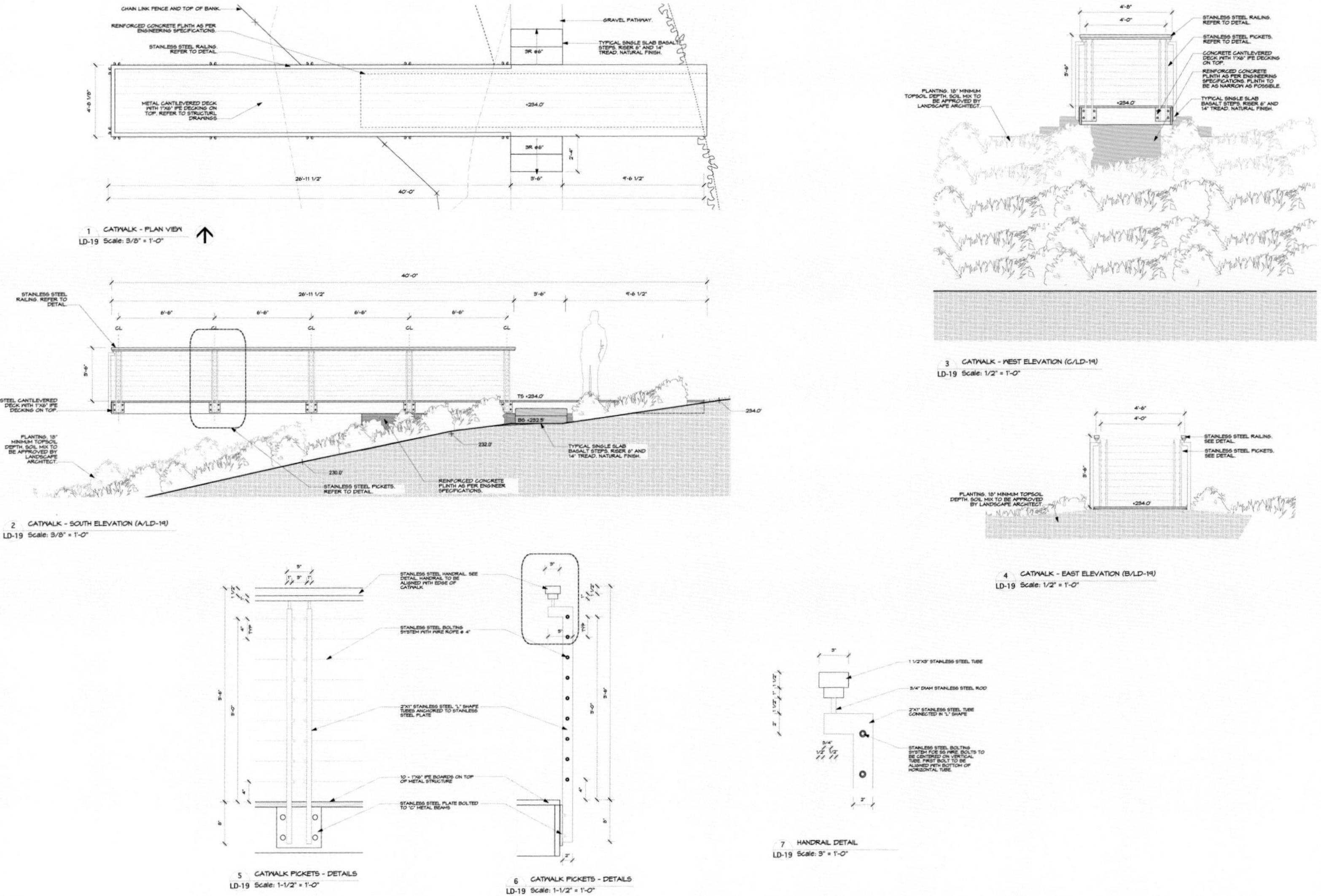

Above. Catwalk details

Next Spread. Viewed from the ravine below, the catwalk is a sensitive addition to the native landscape.

Above. The minimalist stainless steel and airplane wire railing allows light and shadows to dance across the Ipe decking.

Left. The catwalk at the ravine's edge launches from a bed of Oregon Grape (*Mahonia*) into the coniferous forest.

Left. Inspired by an abstract red chandelier in the home's interior, the custom sculpture on the great lawn was designed as a counterpoint to balance the garden architecture.

Right. Sculpture concept development.

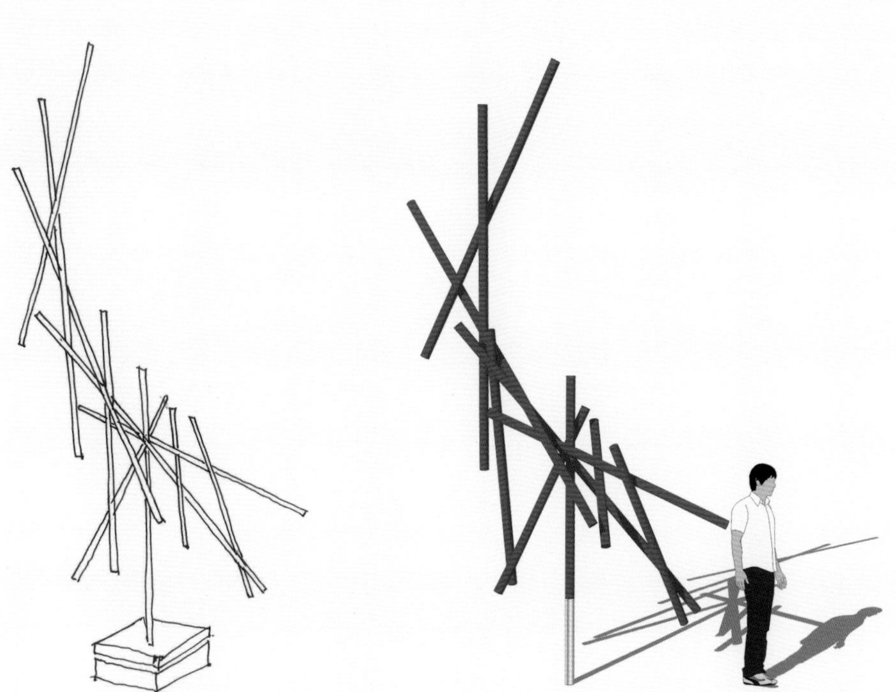

Left. The entry reflecting pool emerges from the lush textural planting.

Above. Ornamental Onion (*Allium*), Plantain Lily (*Hosta*) and Gingko (*Gingko biloba*) create a richly textured, yet appropriately restrained composition.

Left. Rhododendron leaves reach towards the fine blooms of Ornamental Onion (*Allium*).

Next Spread. A timeless tapestry of water, pebbles, slate and planting.

Left. At the southeast corner of the great lawn, specimen Red Japanese Maple (*Acer palmatum* 'Atropurpureum') and Mount Fuji Cherry (*Prunus serrulata 'Mount Fuji'*) frame a water feature flanked by local basalt boulders.

Above. Past a waterfall, a pathway of refined stepping stones floats across the surface of the water feature.

Left. A vegetable garden of the kitchen captures the last rays of sunlight.

Above. Architecture and landscape articulate and define space.

Left. Crisp, architectural stairs contrast the organic forms and textural plantings.

Right. Soft layers of texture and colour envelop the crisp forms of the principal residence.

BEFORE & AFTER

CRAFTING

3. CLUB HOUSE

The garden at Clubhouse appears to emerge as a natural outgrowth of the landscape. Basalt, a local stone that clads both the house and the landscape walls, was carefully selected and placed to appear timeless and organic, with weathered sides facing out and a grey palette that compliments the soft, diffused Vancouver light. The design's sensitivity to form, material, and colour strengthens the connection between the architecture and a nearby ravine, which dramatically cuts through the site, bifurcating the property.

The clubhouse—an additional living space that is connected by bridge to the main property—sits on the site's highest point and receives the most sun, making it a place for summer pilgrimage. Indeed, a pool, a tennis court, and areas to spectate provide lively spaces to soak in the sun. The pool, fed by open pipes inspired by farmer's irrigation canals, stretches out like a well-watered field in front of the clubhouse. The pool lies on axis with an outdoor kitchen that is equipped with a pizza oven and a large stone table. A Magnolia-lined (*Magnolia grandiflora*) tennis court lays three meters below the grade of the clubhouse, offering a bird's eye view of the play from the building.

A subtle progression in planting style flows through the site: from textural plants, like ferns and maples (*Acer circinatum*), on the northwest side, to Tuscan-inspired vegetation, like lavender (*Lavandula*) and olive trees, on the south. With a history that seems to exceed it, the garden feels like a well-kept secret.

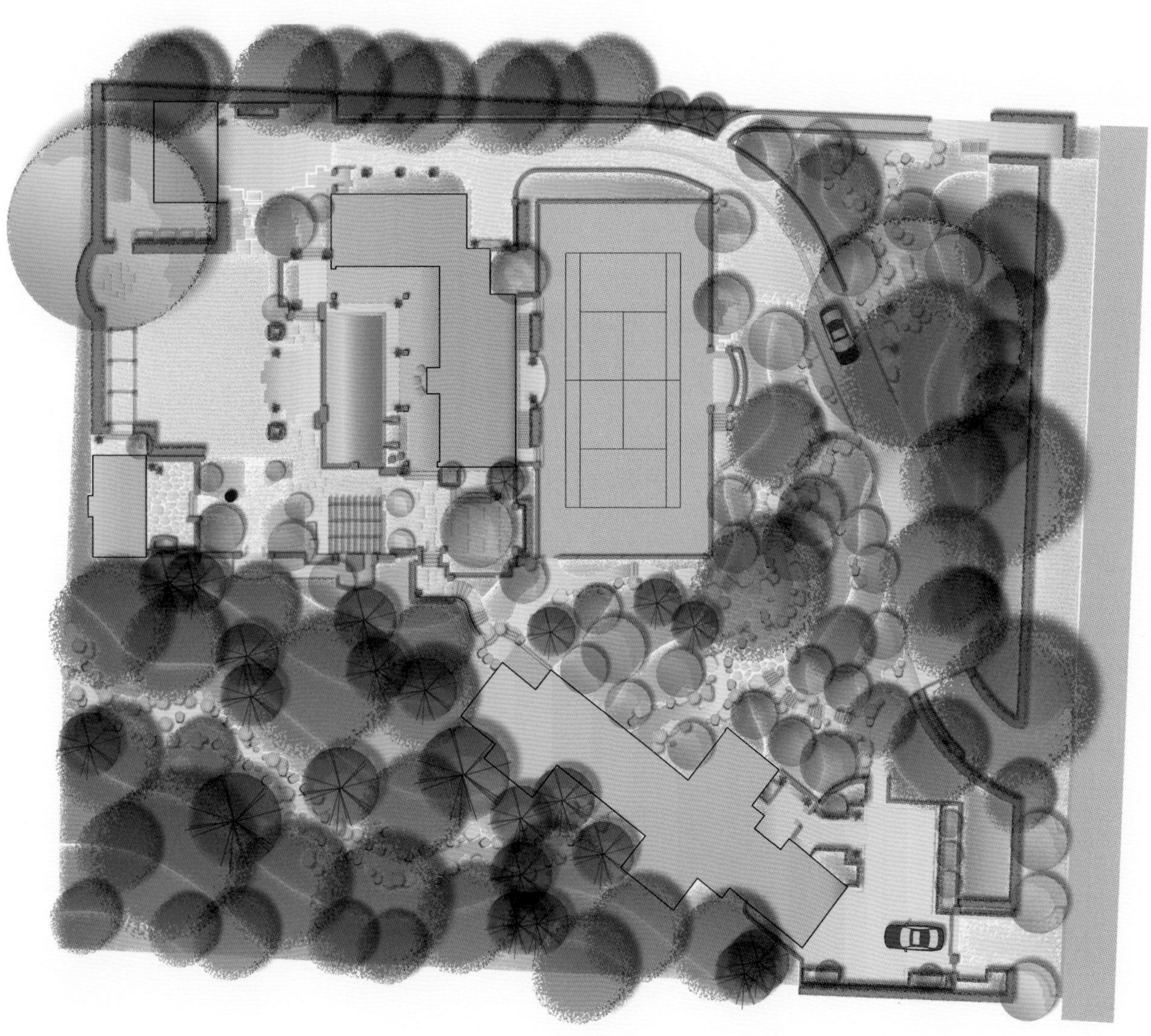

Above. Lenten Rose (*Helleborus*) and Hart's Tongue Fern (*Asplenium scolopendrium*) frame the stone slab steps leading from the residence to the ravine.

Above Right. A tranquil terrace is nestled into the ravine.

Left. Cast iron pots frame the entry garden while a pathway draws the eye towards the landscape beyond.

Left and Above. Handrail and basalt steps thread through lush vegetation to the ravine below.

Right. Sculptural metal railings draw inspiration from the form of the surrounding trees.

Above. In the ravine, shadow and light silhouette Vine Maple (Acer cicinatum) branches.

Left. Light filters through the forest canopy, creating jewel-like patterns on the creek below.

Next Spread. False Spiraea (Astilbe) and Burning Bush (Eunymus) cascade across a basalt path with planted joints of Baby's Tears (Soleirolia soleirolii).

Above. An existing bridge arches gracefully over the creek, framing the waterfall behind.

Left. Lush planting frames a suspended living space that links the main residence buildings.

Next Spread. Symmetrical stone stairs spill down from the overview to the tennis court while lush vines climb the basalt-clad wall, threading the building and landscape together.

Above. Stone cobbles define the plantings through the gravel driveway.

Above Right. Views to the tennis court from the stairwell are filtered through the fine textured foliage of a Honey Locust (*Gleditsia triacanthos*).

Left. Merging from the ravine, rustic stone walls frame the gravel driveway.

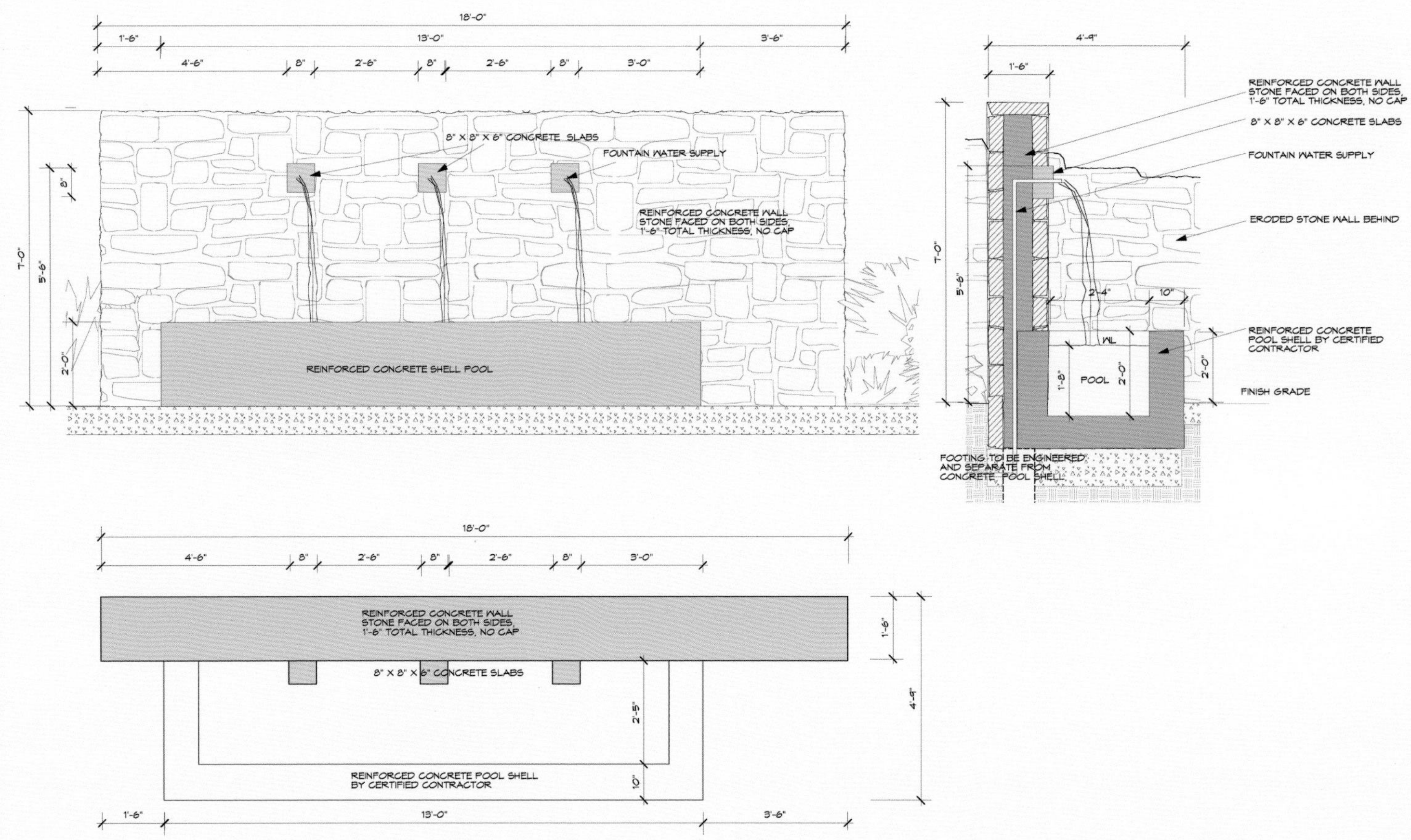

Above. Water trough details.

Right. Natural stone cladding carries from the home into the garden's architectural features. Northwest of the garage, simple copper spigots punctuate the stone wall, spilling water into the crisp concrete trough below.

Above. Water trough in arrival court.

Left. A bluestone path leads past the clubhouse into the garden.

Above. Layered plantings spill on to the bluestone pathway.

Right. A simple palette of Boxwood (*Buxus*), Lavender (*Lavandula*) and Hebe are clipped into sculptural forms that contrast with the lawn and Boxwood (*Buxus*) hedge beyond.

Above. Framing the garden's edge, a pizza oven, grape clad trellis and stone table provide a backdrop for the slate-lined swimming cistern.

Above. Framed by Peegee Hydrangea (*Hydrangea paniculata*), a seating terrace provides lounging at lawn level.

Next Spread. Under the protective cover of the clubhouse veranda, views to the south entice the senses.

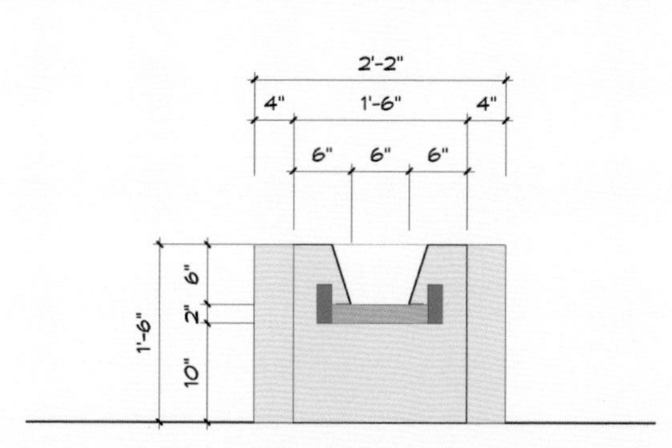

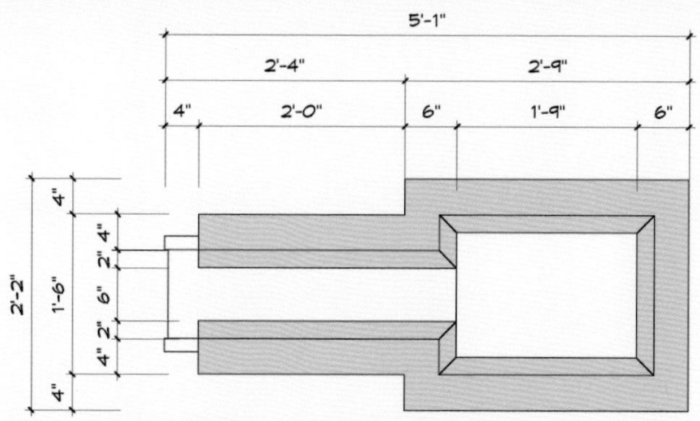

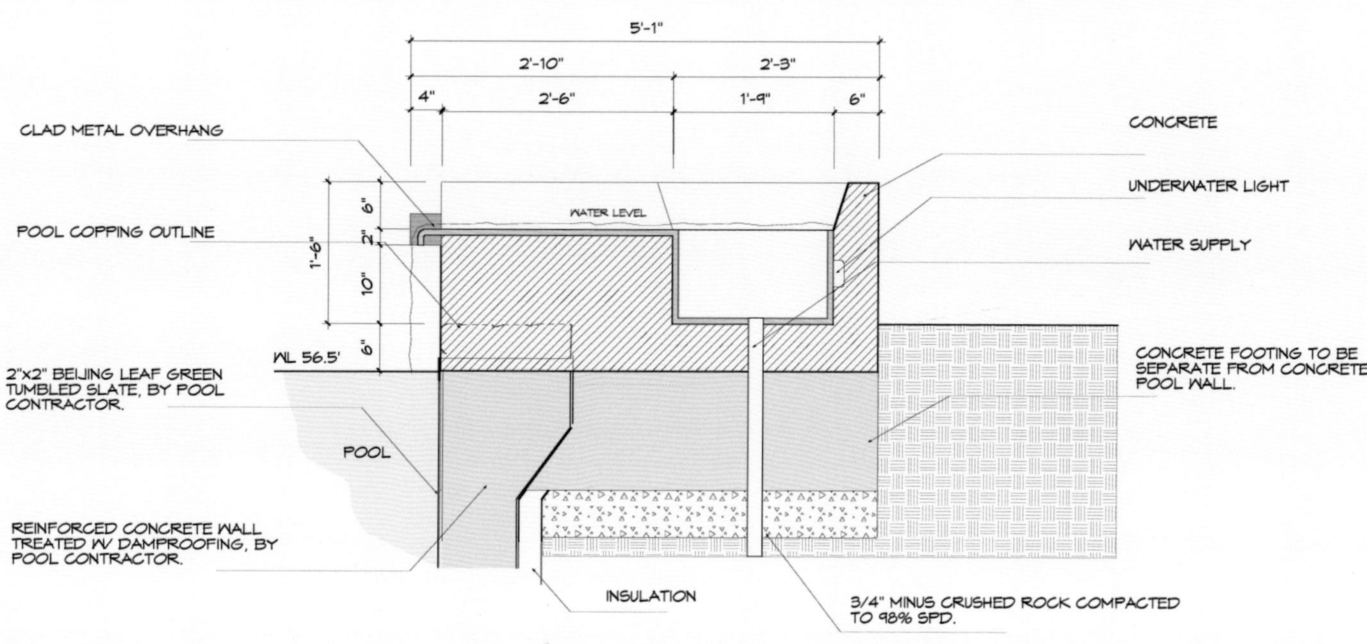

Above. Water spout detail.

Next Spread. Arriving from the main residence, the light, water, textures and planting provide a rich tapestry.

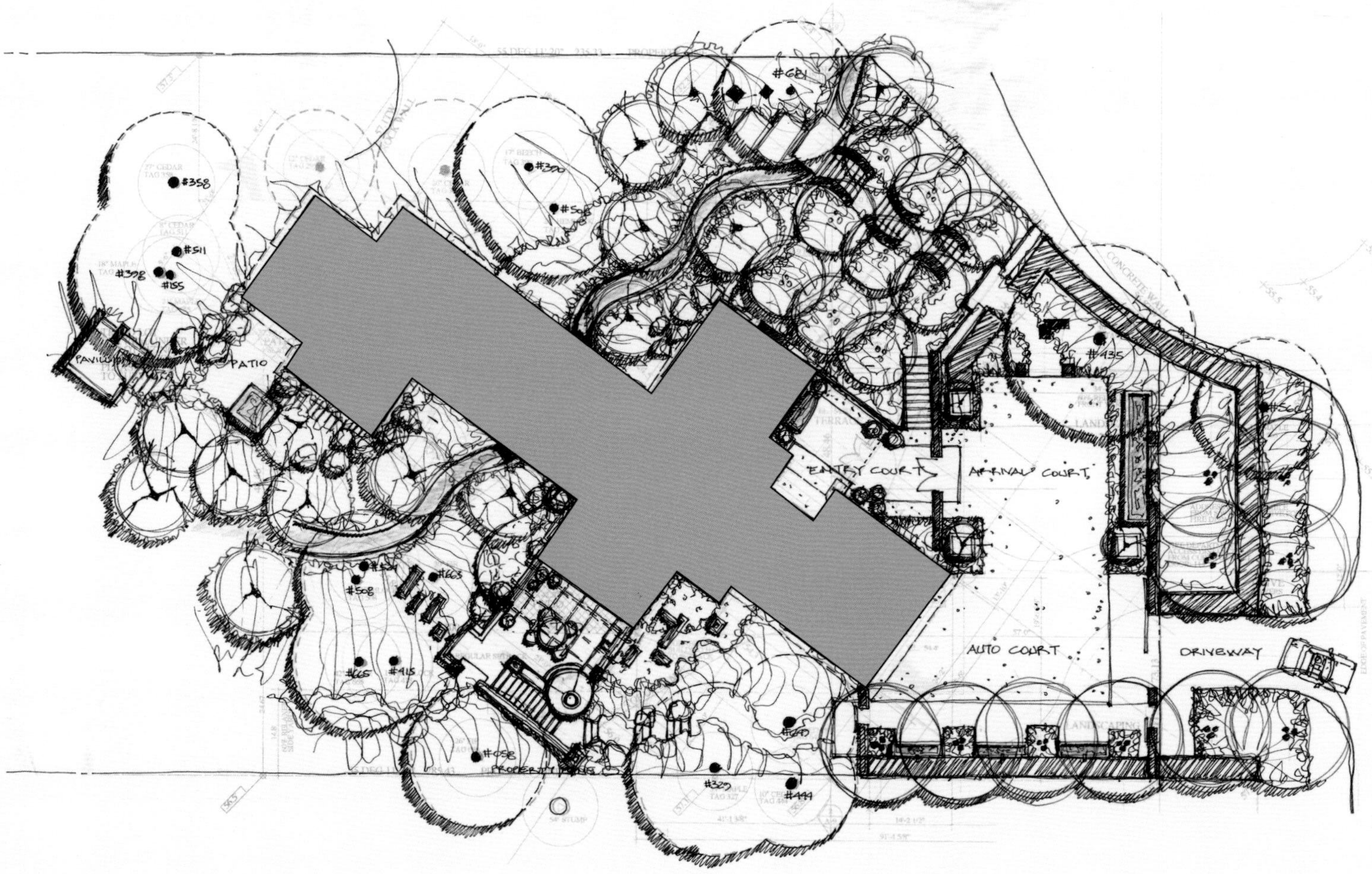

Above. Conceptual master plan and wall details.

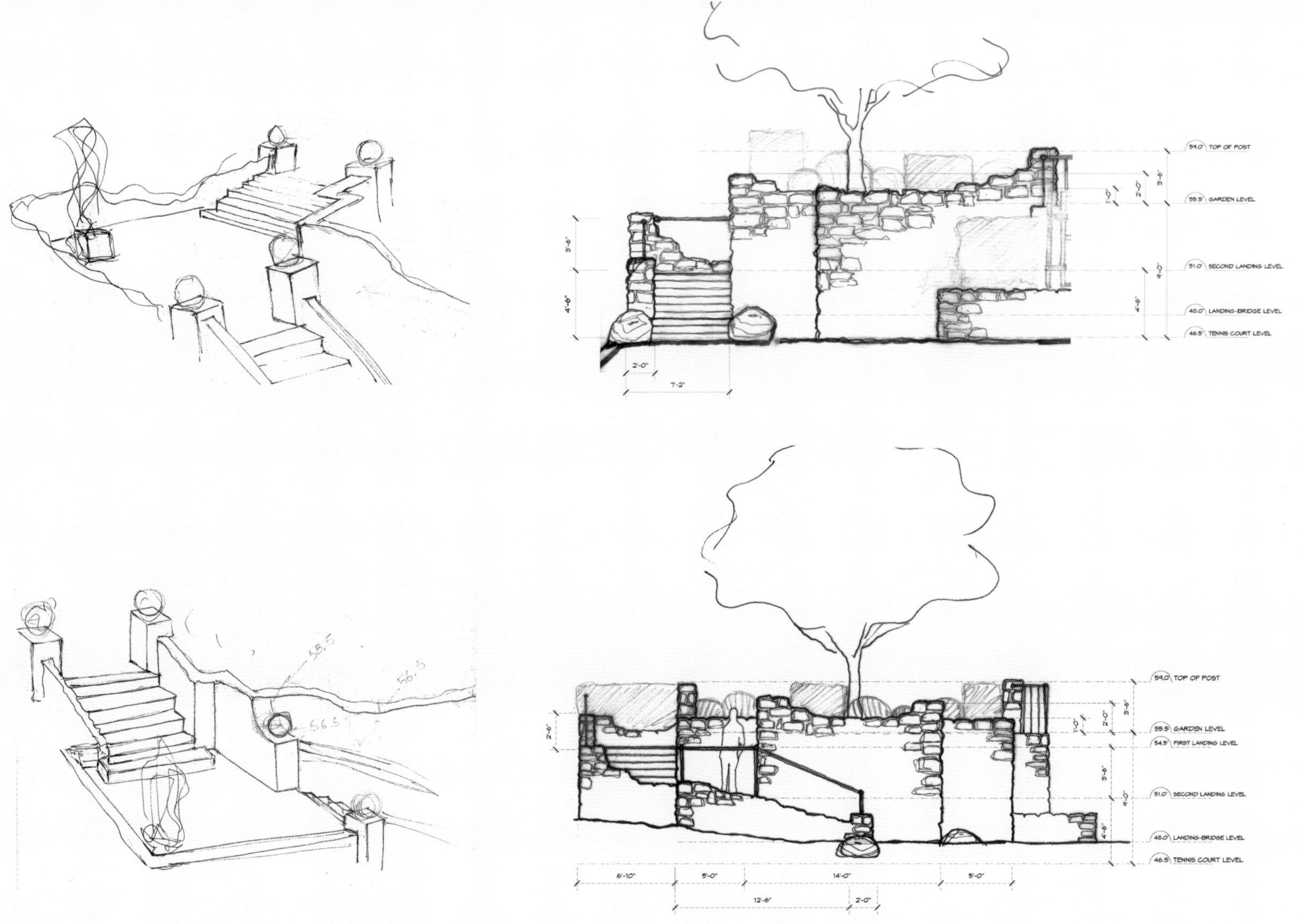

Next Spread. Lush, exuberant planting frames and defines the garden's rooms, while embracing the architecture of the clubhouse.

Above. Hand forged ironwork stands in contrast to the green textural plantings behind.

Right. Architecture, planting and ironwork erode and intertwine, linking home and garden on both the horizontal and vertical planes.

Left. Planting and architectural forms complement and contrast with each other in a lush garden vignette.

Right. The path to the studio is defined by a Grape Vine (*Vitis vinifera*) covered pergola.

Above. A gravel path weaves its way through sculptural planted forms from the studio to the clubhouse.

Right. The Southern Catalpa (*Catalpa bignoniodes*) punctures through a bed of clipped Boxwood (*Buxus*) hedging, providing a visual anchor for the surrounding space.

Left. The setting sun highlights the ravine trees which frame the garden.

Above. The gravel path leads the eye across the sun-dappled lawn to the stable beyond.

Left. Boxwood (*Buxus*) frames the lawn terrace connecting the studio to the arrival court.

Right. Existing Southern Catalpa (*Catalpa bignoniodes*) is silhouetted by the setting sun.

Next Spread. The stone tile pool captures the last rays of a summer sunset.

BEFORE & AFTER

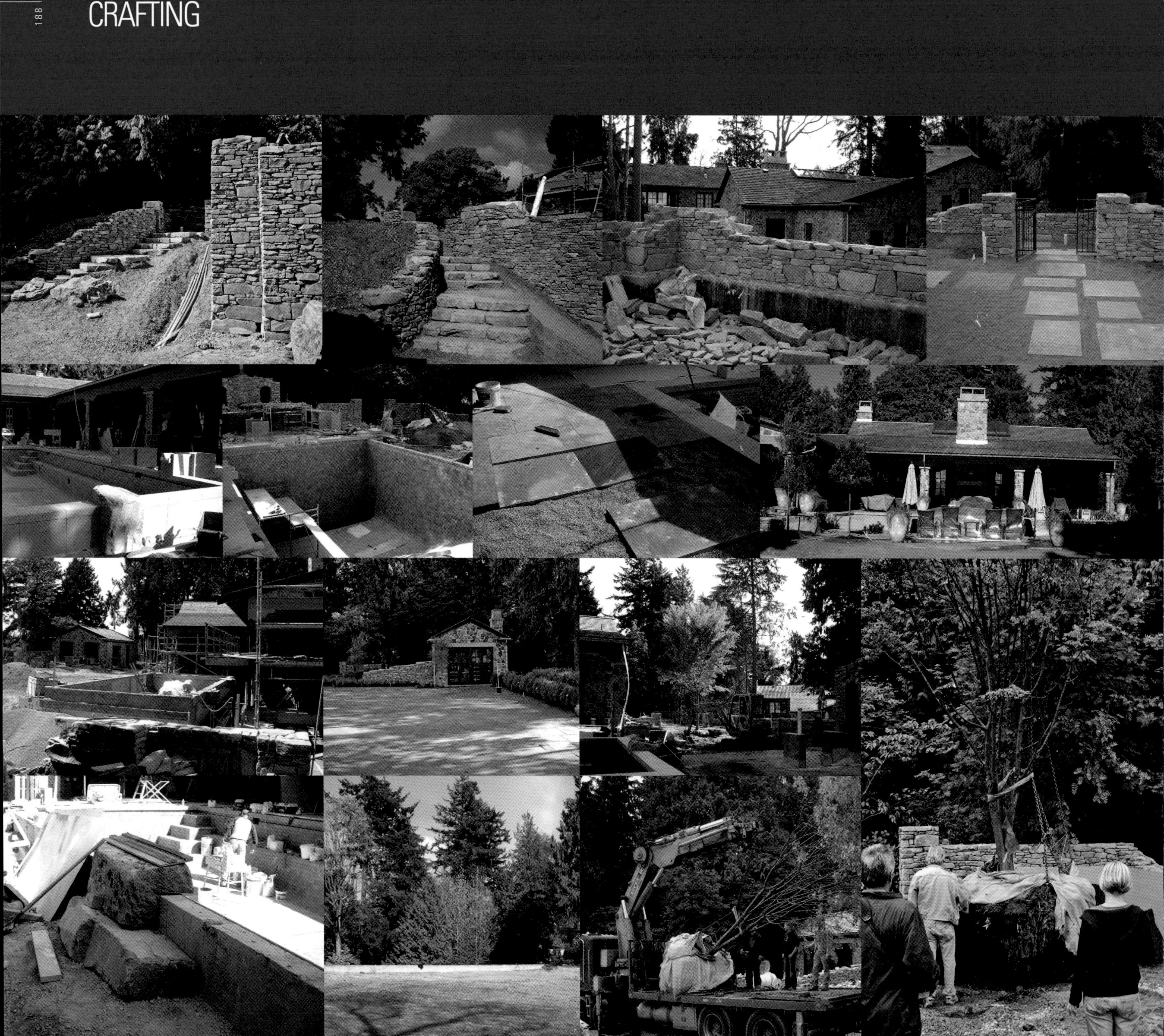

4. CREEK'S END

Creek's End is a tapestry of subtle beach pebble grays, textured rainforest-inspired planting and glimmering reflective surfaces. As an abstraction of the natural transition of the west coast landscape at its dynamic nexus of mountain and sea, the design is anchored by a series of terraces softened by channels of textural planting and rivulets of moving water. With its foreshore improvements and re-naturalization of a culverted stream within a public right of way, Creek's End enriches its social and ecological context while providing a uniquely west coast sanctuary for its owners.

Framed by an inviting arbor, abstract branch forms of the front entry gate welcome visitors into the intimate entry court, referencing the site's mountain backdrop. A focal water feature animates the entry garden, with a bridge providing access to the home's front door. Reflecting the movement of the adjacent creek, water spills from the central feature downward through the garden terraces, drawing users towards the garden rooms on the lower floor. The path from the entry courtyard to foreshore is marked by a subtle evolution from the architectural to the natural. Juxtaposing the terraces' contemporary formal structure with roughly textured local basalt boulders and naturalistic planting, the site expresses a sensitive relationship between the organic and the abstract.

The diffused grey hardscape palette of bluestone and basalt blends seamlessly with the pebbled public foreshore beyond. Strategic placement of boulders, logs and planting encourages natural sediment deposition, improving the habitat while protecting the site from extreme storm events. Adjacent to the residence, a public right of way that previously contained an asphalt access road with a culverted stream below has been transformed into a naturalized stream and winding pedestrian path with naturalistic planting. The salmon-bearing creek now flows naturally, enriching the site with invaluable habitat.

Creek's Edge embraces its position as a landscape of transition, expressing its context through its subtle form, materiality, texture, contrast and connections to the public landscapes beyond.

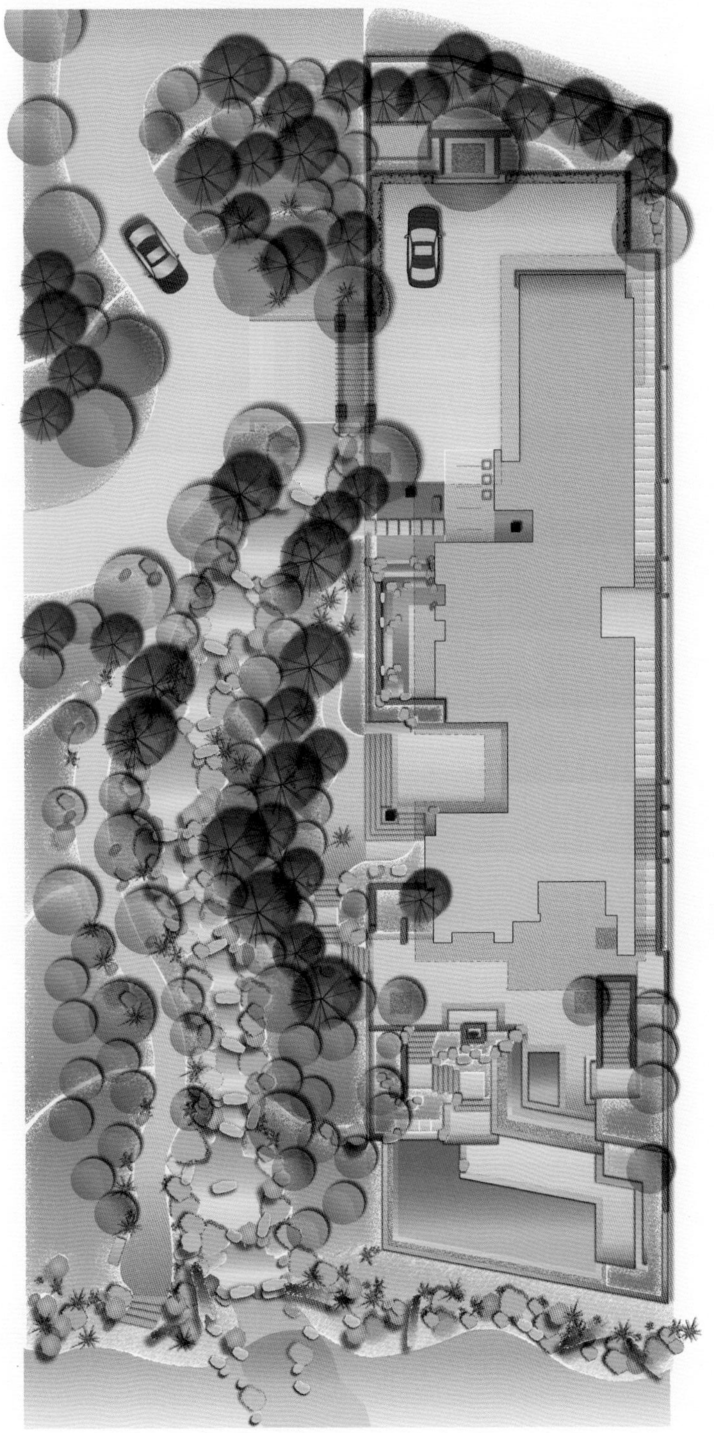

Left. Framed by an inviting arbor, abstract branch forms of the front entry gate welcome visitors into the intimate entry court and speak to the site's contextual and conceptual relationship with nature.

Above Right. The entry gate and arbor define the private residential threshold separating the autocourt from the public access lane. The open metalwork integrates the crisp lines of the residence with the natural forms of the surrounding forest.

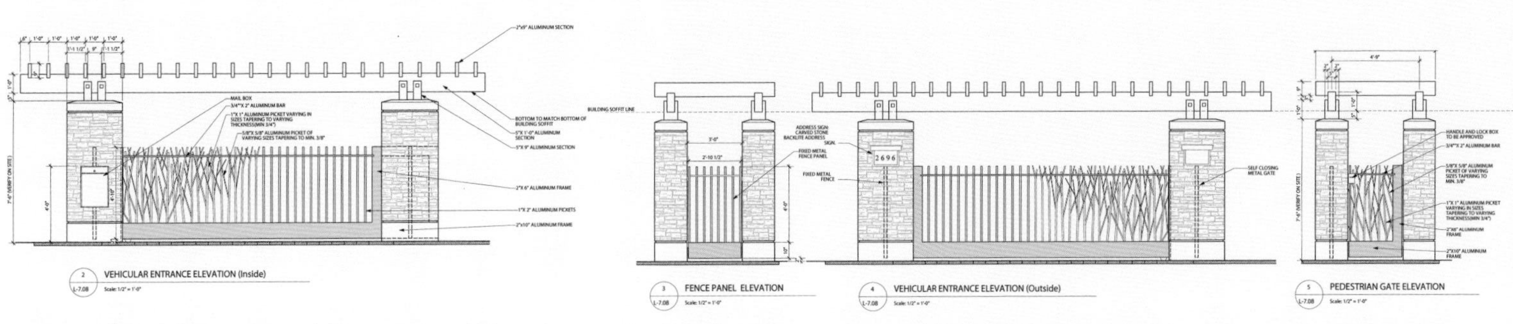

Above. Gate and arbor detail.

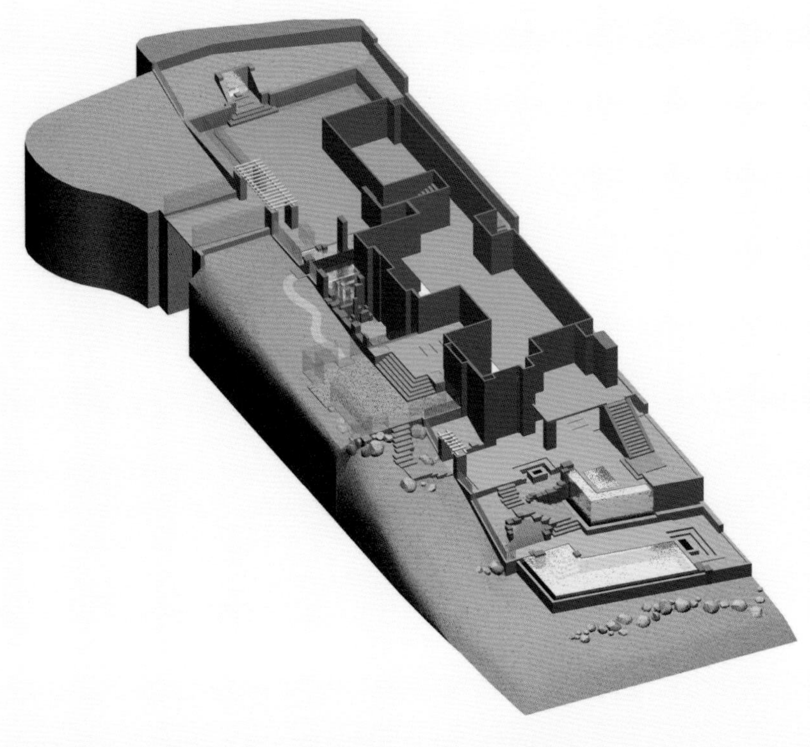

Above. 3D study model.

Left. Articulating the architectural concrete of the auto-court wall provides an alcove for feature planting.

Right. Textures and patterns create playful juxtapositions.

Left. A focal water feature animates the entry garden.

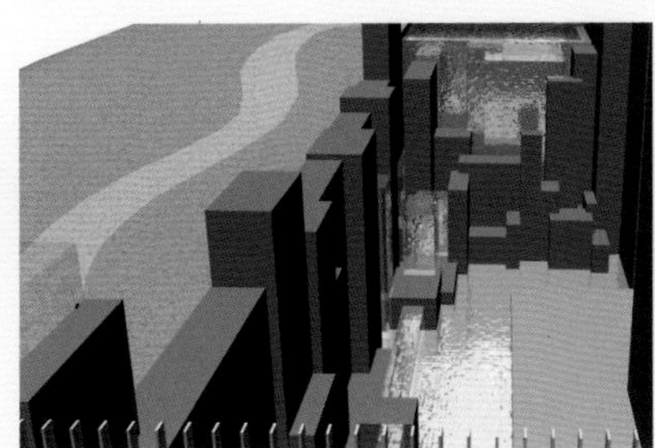

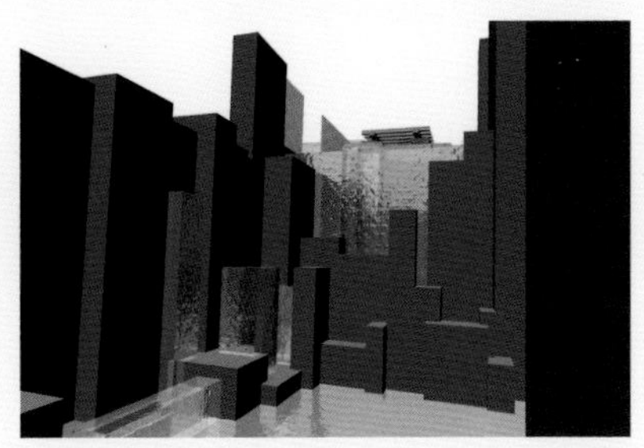

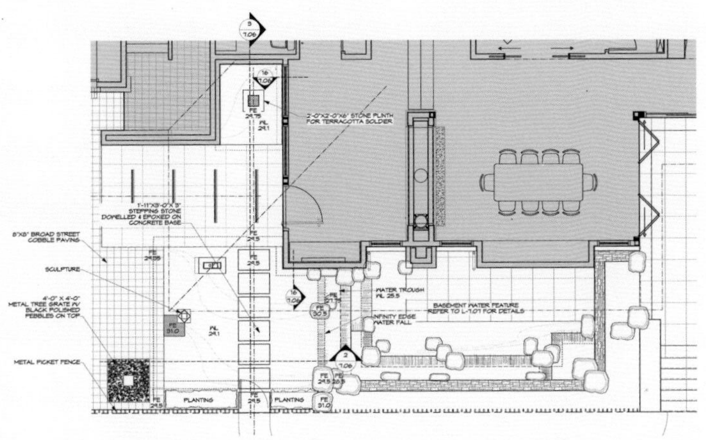

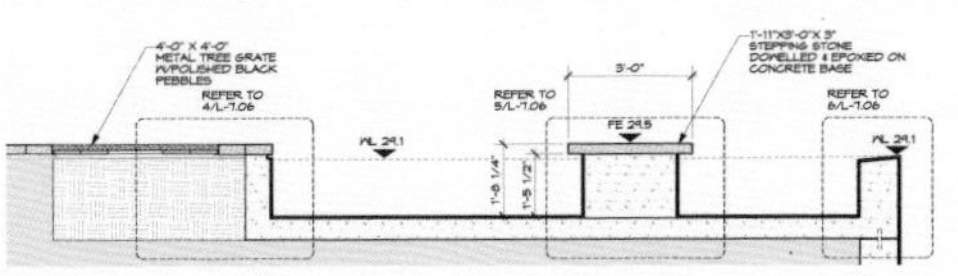

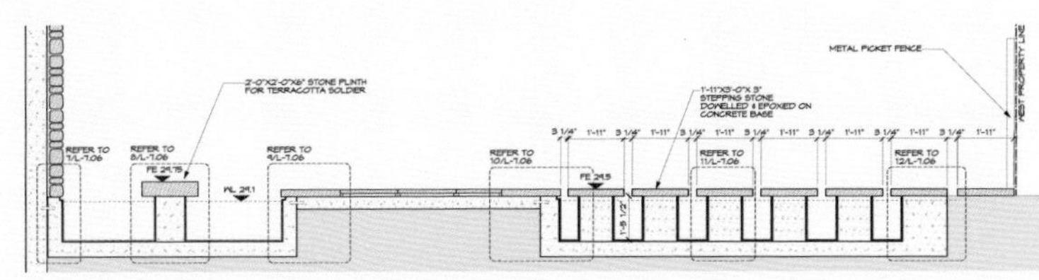

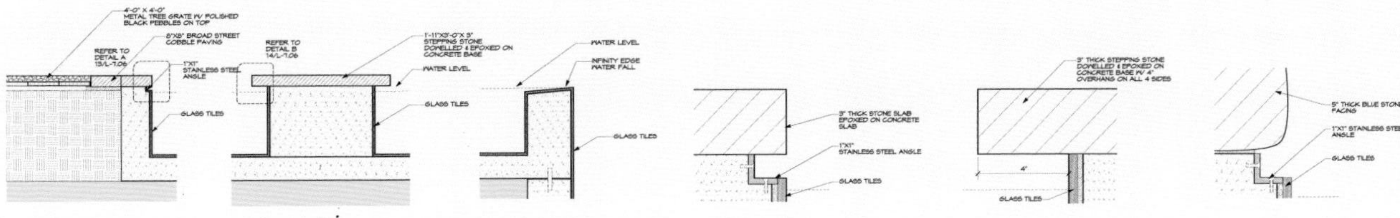

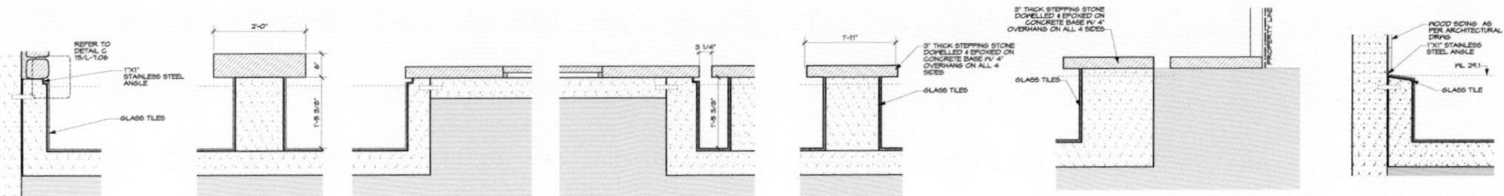

Above. Entry pool details.

Above. Textured planting leads the way to the lower terraces along the west side of the residence.

Above. Naturalized plantings contrast the crisp architectural lines of the stairs.

Above. Stone pavers nestle into walkable plantings of Baby's Tears (*Soleirolia soleiriolii*).

Right. Unstructured paths link the geometric terraces between the creek and residence.

Next Spread. The diffused palette of bluestone, basalt and water blends seamlessly with the ocean and rocky foreshore.

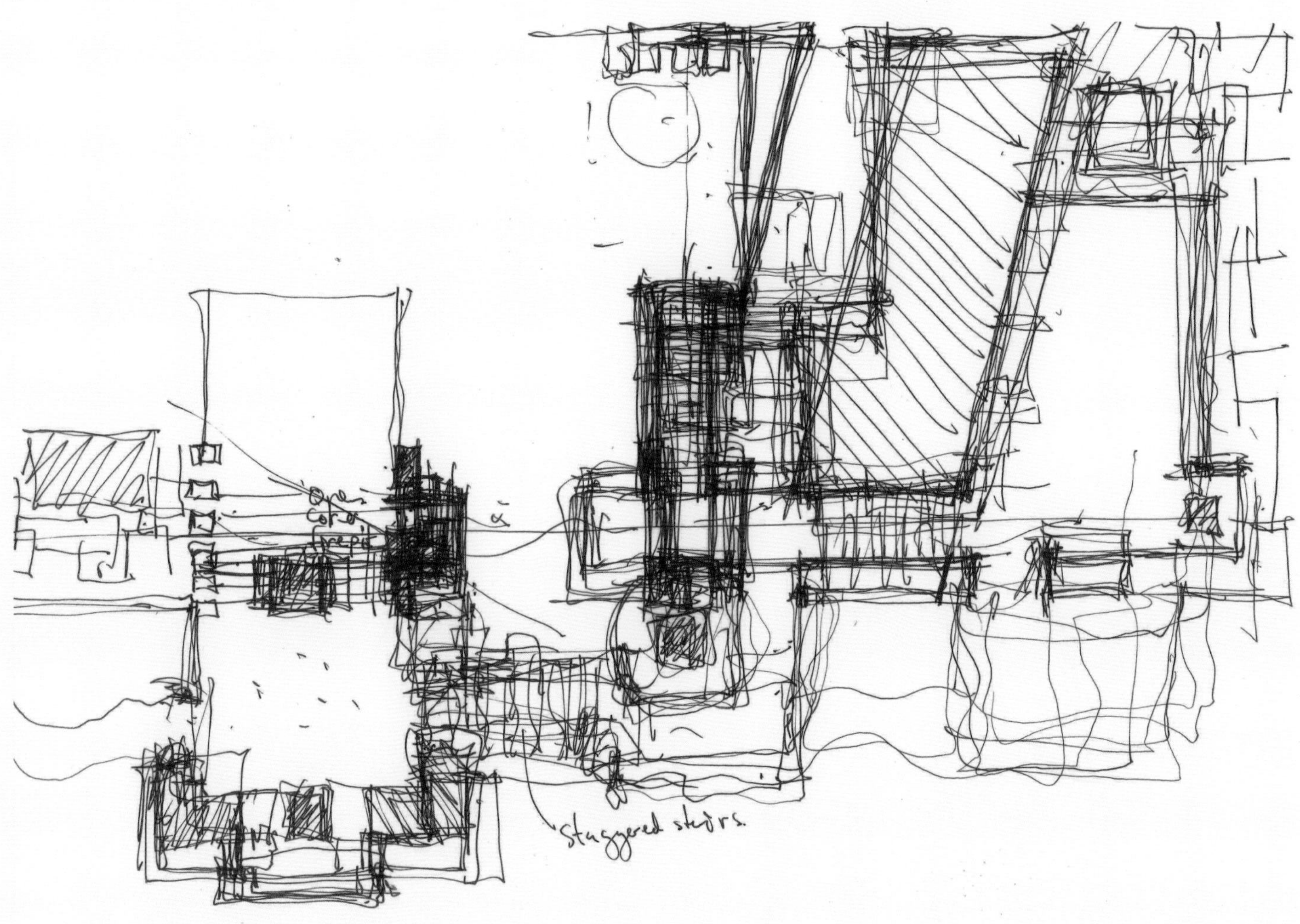

Above. Concept exploration drawing.

Left. A juxtaposition of the organic against the refined, the lower pool terrace links to the beach beyond.

Next Spread. Nestled in the beach grasses, the rectilinear glass tiled pool provides an architectural contrast to the organic.

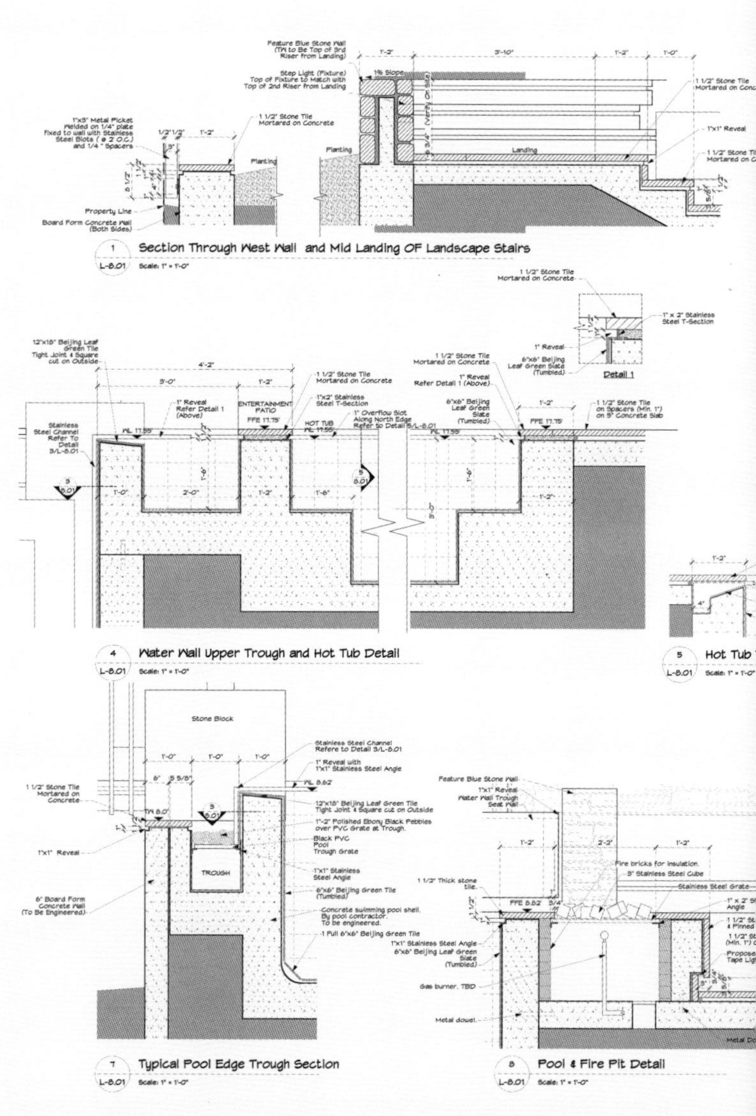

Above. Summer blooms and grasses cascade over the edges of the pool.

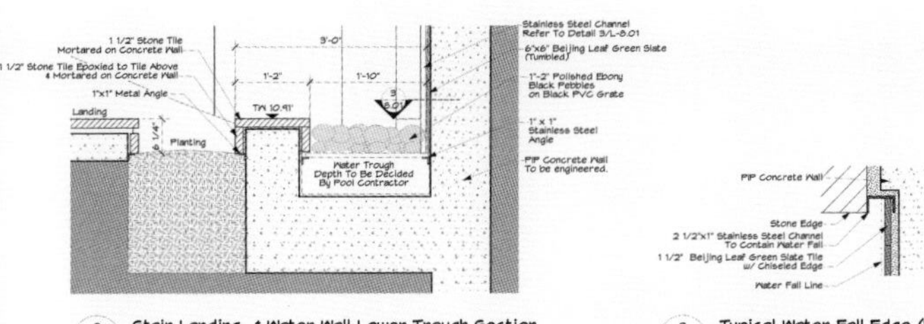

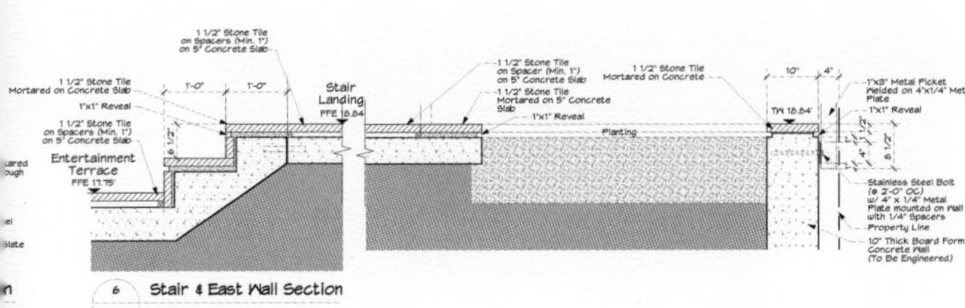

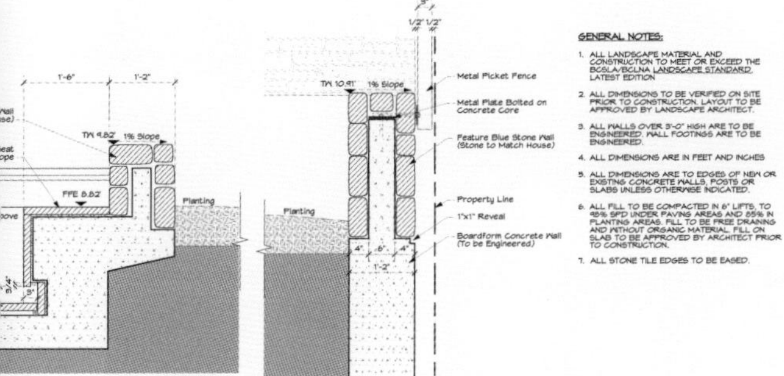

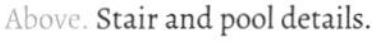

Above. Stair and pool details.

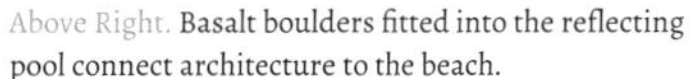

Above Right. Basalt boulders fitted into the reflecting pool connect architecture to the beach.

Above. Subtle contrasts of harmonious colour and texture at the water wall create a sense of balance and serenity.

Right. Ridges in basalt tiles cut water into rivulets as it flows down the wall.

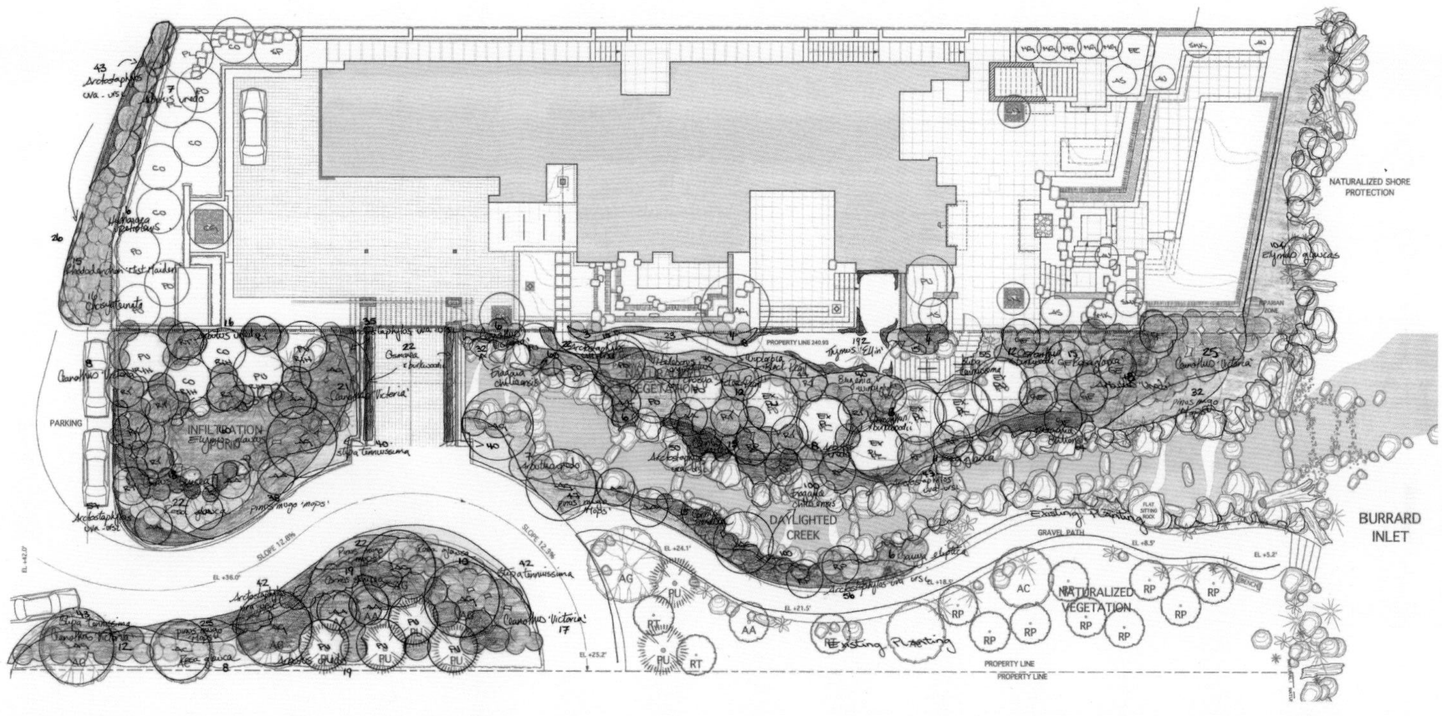

Far Above. Public space planting plan.

Above. Naturalistic planting in the public right of way and foreshore blends seamlessly with the private landscape.

Above. The daylighted creek provides valuable habitat, while a gravel path provides an inviting public access to the beach.

Right and Next Spread. Planting, logs and boulders on the foreshore create valuable habitat and protect the site from the damaging effects of extreme storm events.

BEFORE & AFTER

5. TSAWWASSEN BLUFF

Though Tsawwassen, a garden for a grand French château-inspired home on an ocean-facing bluff, is influenced by classical French gardens, the design offers a fresh, contemporary take on formal arrangement and composition. The design pays heed to one of the most important tenets of French formal landscape design: axial views create the framework of the work's spatial organization. A tapered allée of Leprechaun Ash trees (*Fraxinus pennsylvanica 'Johnson'*) encased by a *parterre de broderie* of boxwood presents a forced perspective from an outdoor kitchen patio to an eyecatcher—a large, elevated urn. A perpendicular axis reaches from a parterre with a Magnolia tree (*grandiflora*) in its center to the indefinite distance of an open view of the ocean and the far off mountains, the view perfectly framed by Douglas Fir trees (*Pseudotsuga menziesii*).

Although axes give a strong sense of rational order to the landscape, the whimsy, sinuous shapes of the planting beds and paths transgress the strict geometry, slowing down the pace of the walk and encouraging one to smell, touch, look, and listen. The design of Tsawwassen is classic proof of the axiom, "Know the rules well, so you can break them effectively." Serpentine walkways wind around the property, through a fernery, shade garden, and a grove of Redwood, offering a slew of experiences and sensory pleasures. In the center of the circular driveway a large planter of lavender gives a sweet-smelling greeting. Just outside the home office rests a contemplative rock garden—a sculptural miniaturization of the distant mountains.

In addition to designing apertures for the scenery, the design also strategically orchestrates moments with expansive views of the house, particularly along the periphery of the garden. Because of the landscape's axial relationship to the home's architecture—especially to its windows and doors—the garden comes into sharp focus from inside of the home.

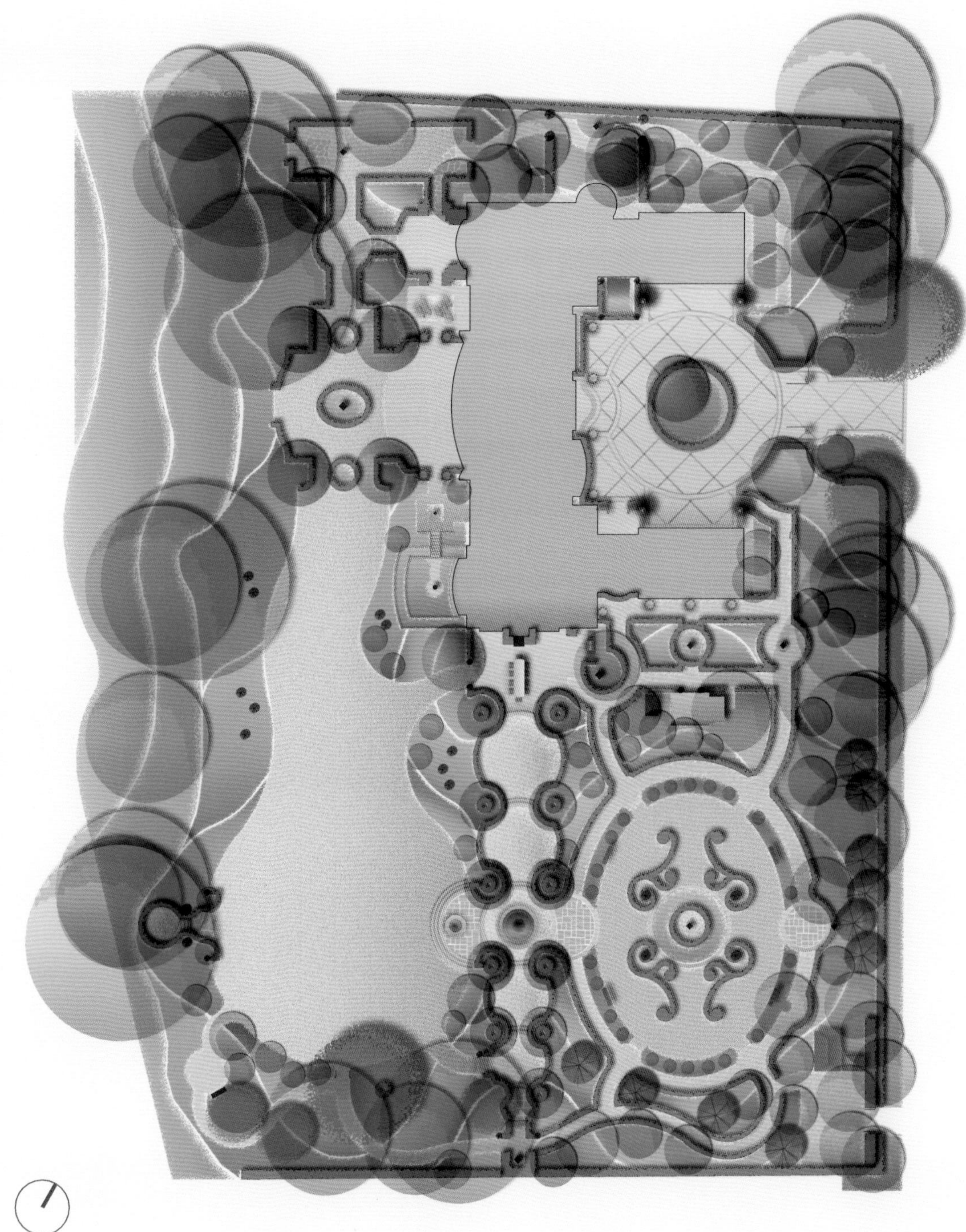

Left. Persian Ironwood (*Parrotia persica*), Ornamental Onion (*Allium*), and Boxwood (*Buxus*) create a whimsical and dramatic entry.

Above. Ornamental Onion (*Allium*) flowers float over Lavender (*Lavandula*) blooms.

Above. A layered understorey anchors the Douglas Fir (*Pseudotsuga menziesii*) to the formal garden.

Next Spread. Boxwood (*Buxus*) parterres define lawn edges and architecturally connect the residence to the bluff.

Left. A sculpture of Mercury provides a focal point to the dining terrace.

Above. The living terrace echoes the form of the architecture as well as the circular parterres on the adjacent lawn.

Next Spread. Providing scale to the view, sculpture, garden and terrace unite.

Previous Spread. Boxwood (*Buxus*) parterres and voluminous perenials mediate the transition between architecture and lawn.

Left. Speaking to both the classical and contemporary elements of the residence, rectilinear Corten retaining walls structure a sunken boxwood garden.

Right. Douglas Fir (*Pseudotsuga menziesii*) frame views to the west beyond the Boxwood (*Buxus*) parterres.

Left. Catmint (*Nepeta*) lines the edge of the finely maintained lawn.

Right. Douglas Fir (*Pseudotsuga menziesii*) and the perennial/shrub border define the cultivated garden and the naturalized embankment.

Above. The forced perspective of the Ash (*Fraxinus*) allee provides a dramatic separation between the lawn terrace and rose garden.

Right. The limestone firepit catches the last rays of sunset as they fall across the great lawn.

Below. A layered understorey anchors the Douglas Fir (*Pseudotsuga menziesii*) to the formal garden.

Next Spread. A limestone fountain sits at the intersection of the Ash (*Fraxinus*) allée and rose garden axes. In the evening light, the garden's magical, almost otherworldly quality is fully expressed.

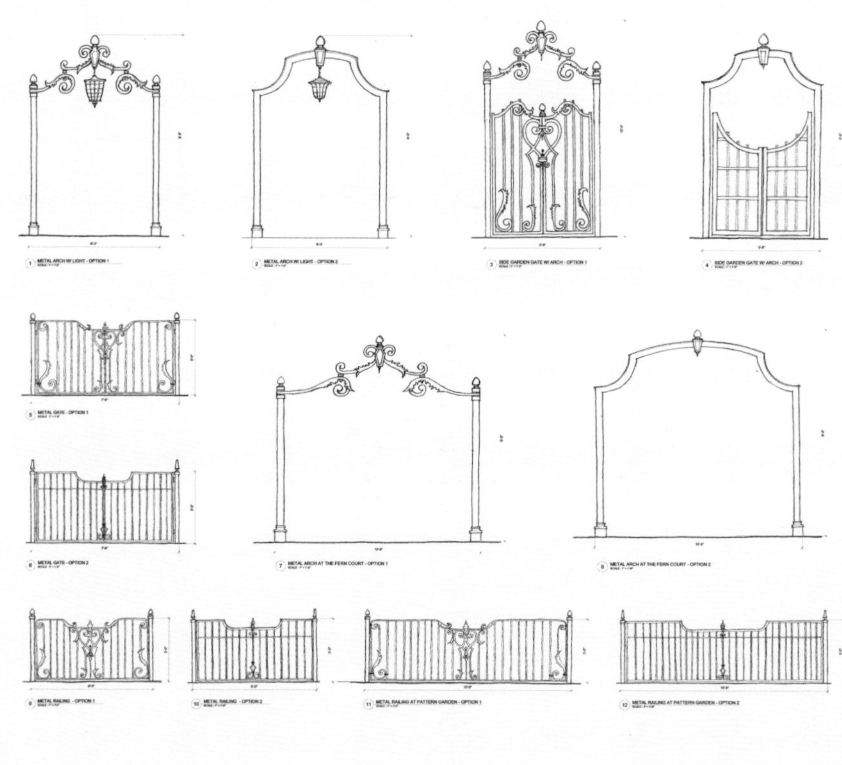

Above. Axial views terminate at finely detailed gates and arches, defining spaces while encouraging exploration.

Above Right. Conceptual gate designs.

Right. Japanese Maple (*Acer palmatum*) 'Bloodgood' leaves.

Next Spread. The firepit and fountain define the cross axis through the Ash (*Fraxinus*) allee to the rose garden and great lawn.

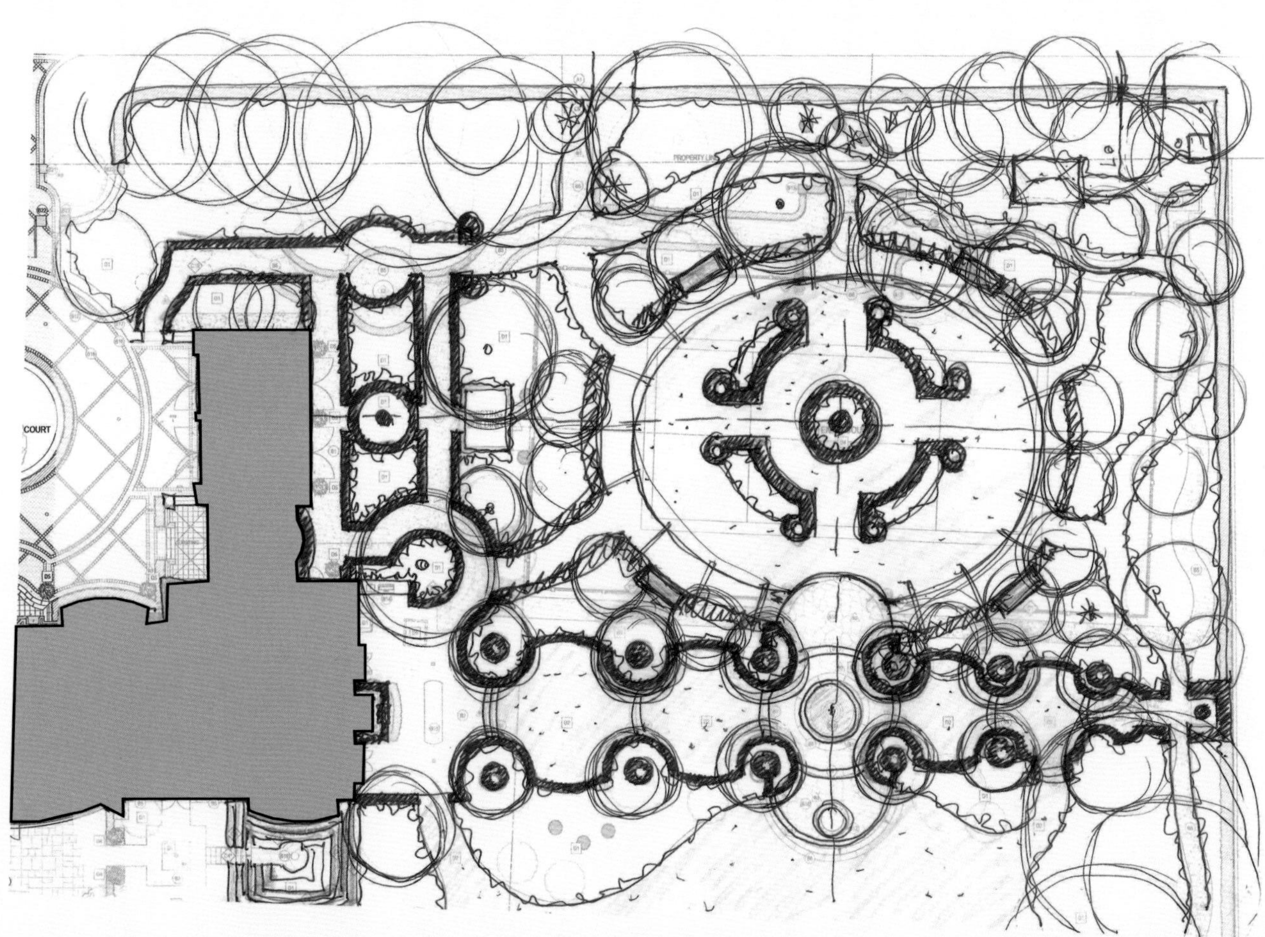

Above. Rose garden concept.

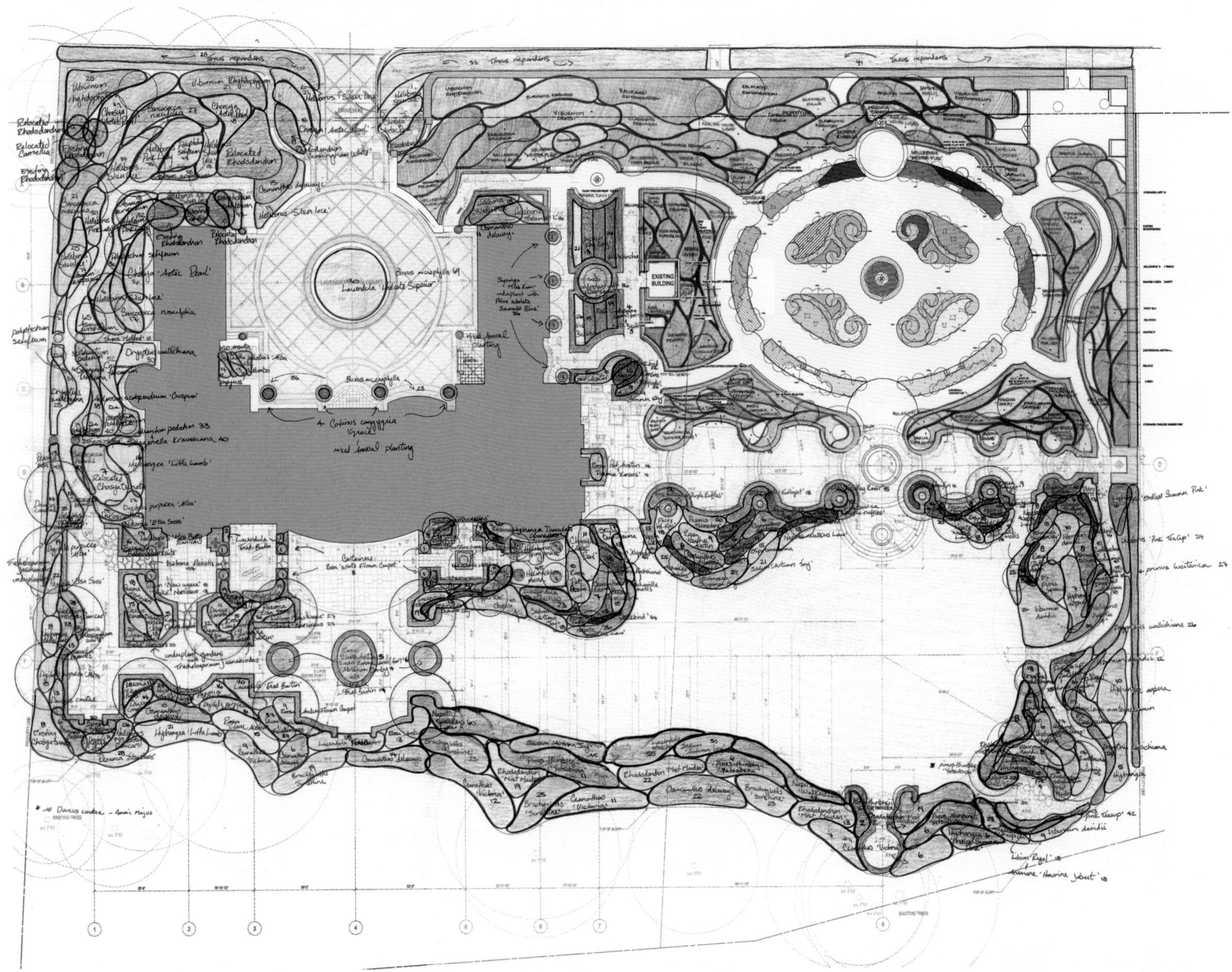

Above. Planting Plan.

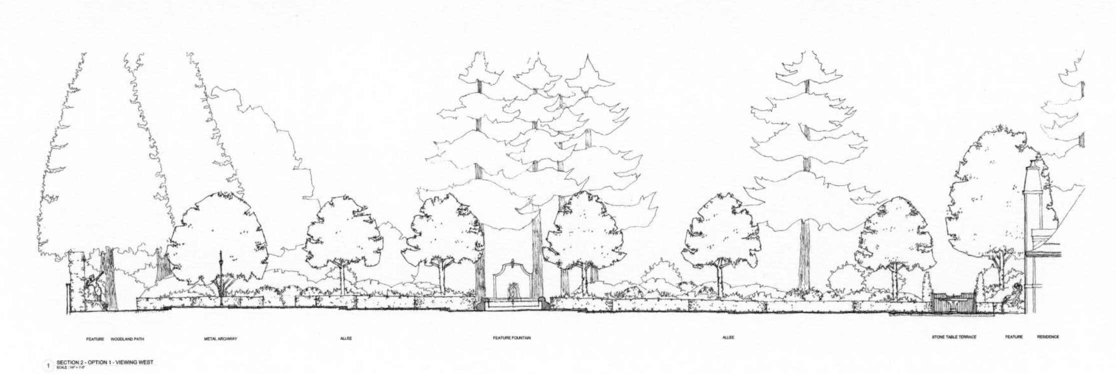

Left. Leprechaun Ash (*Fraxinus pennsylvanica 'Johnson'*) reinforce the perspective of the allée and central fountain.

Above. The garden glows in the evening summer sunlight. The feathery leaves of Golden Robinia (*Robinia pseudoacacia 'Frisia'*) accentuate the golden glow.

Above. Set on the Ash (*Fraxinus*) allée axis, a limestone table provides for a dramatic dining setting.

Right. A Golden Robinia (*Robinia pseudoacacia 'Frisia'*) provides a finely textured midground for a bespoke limestone dining table.

Left. The central water feature and Ash (*Fraxinus*) allée are framed by the burgundy leaves of Smoke Bush (*Cotinus coggygria*).

Above. Boxwood (*Buxus suffruticosa*) define the planting beds of the Ash (*Fraxinus*) allée.

Left. A large limestone urn provides a focal point in the lush plantings of Kousa Dogwood (*Cornus kousa*) and Hydrangea.

Above. Ash (*Fraxinus*) leaves juxtapositioned over Golden Robinia (*Robinia pseudoacacia 'Frisia'*).

Above. A curvilinear crushed basalt walkway leads around an existing Magnolia to the rose garden.

Above. Rose garden and the Ash (*Fraxinus*) allée are backdropped by Douglas Fir (*Pseudotsuga menziesii*) on the bluff.

Right. A limestone urn and pavers with planted joints define a moment to pause along a garden path.

BEFORE & AFTER

6. UNFOLDED

The front, street-facing garden of Crescent is understated; functioning mainly to showcase the house and bring depth to the space; however in the back, the garden takes full command of the scene.

Looking out from the center of the entertainment terrace, the eye is first drawn to a low-lying sculpture of a rumpled dress resting on the lip of an infinity edge pool. The eye then travels outward along an axis that punctures through a swathe of vegetation to unveil another sculpture, an abstract representation of a stack of snowballs. A third sculpture, a compelling arrangement of red steel beams, stands on the lawn across from the swimming pool. The dramatic work provides a necessary counterbalance to the visual weight and structure of the pool and its pavilion.

Inspired by the sculpture of the dress, hedges of Osmanthus Boxwood (Buxus) are arranged in interlocking folded forms and encase beds of annuals, whose colour palette changes yearly depending on the mood and taste of the client. The boldly coloured annuals lead the eye through the landscape and serve to define the spaces of the garden, including the entertainment terrace, dining terrace, and pool area. The metaphor of fabric continued beyond the hedges; the planting scheme around the western edge of the garden is designed to evoke shimmering silk, with radiant waves of Corsican Lenten Rose (*Helleborus argutfolius*) and False Spiraea (*Astilbe 'Elizabeth van Veen'*), undulating in a vegetative current that starts at the house and extinguishes at the pool pavilion. A crushed basalt path snakes through the matrix of dense vegetation, weaving under limbed up Rhododendron and the dazzling canopy of European Beech trees (*Fagus sylvatica*).

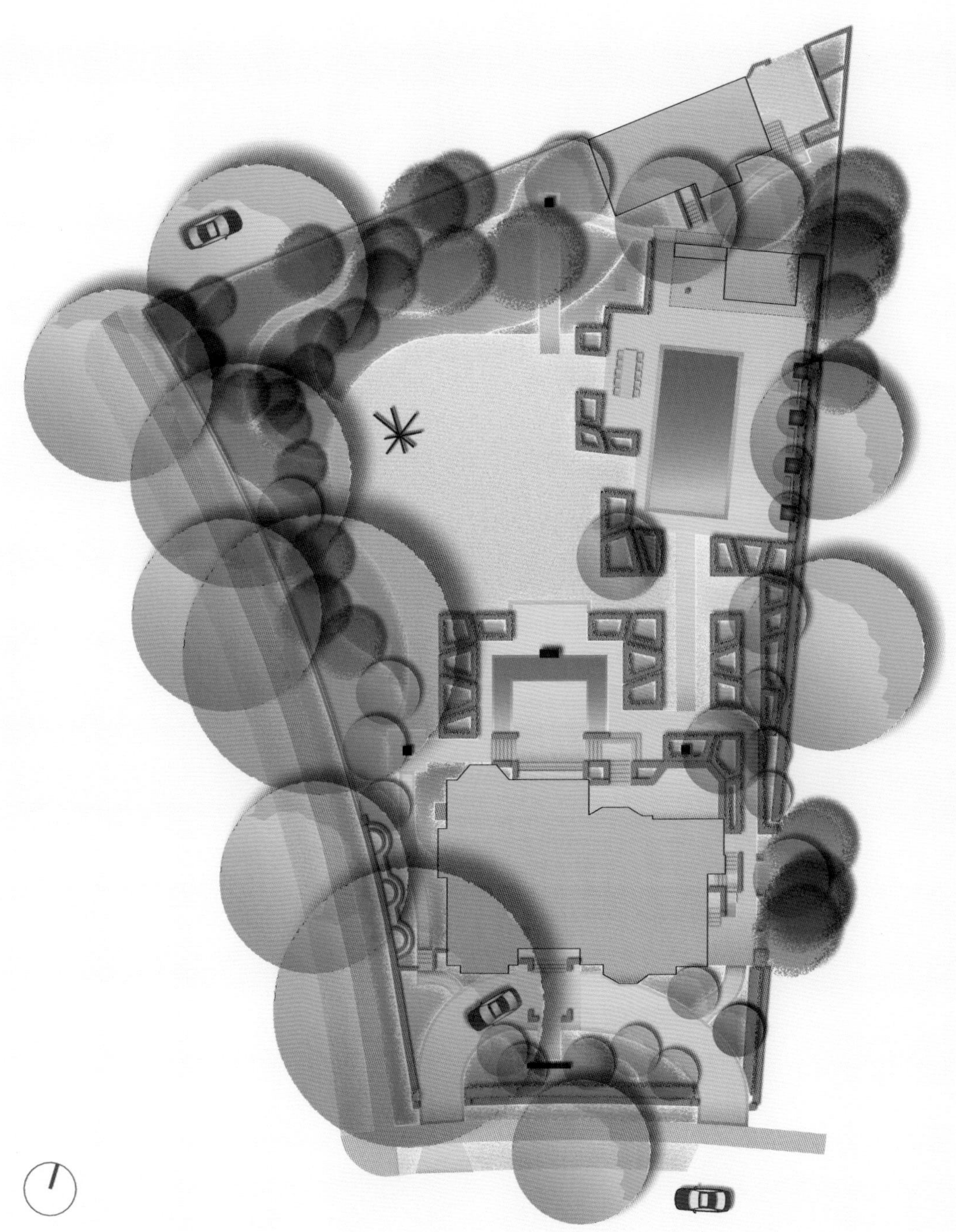

Left. Local Haddington limestone slabs under the porte cochere reinforce the axial relationship between the sculpture that inspired the garden's concept and the front door of the residence.

Right. The folded fabric metaphor that guided the garden's design was drawn from the folds of the Gathie Falk sculpture.

Above. Mimicking the Japanese Maple (*Acer palmatum*) branches, a red abstract sculpture by John Henry.

Left. The entertainment terrace provides a point of prospect from which to view the garden's sculptural planting.

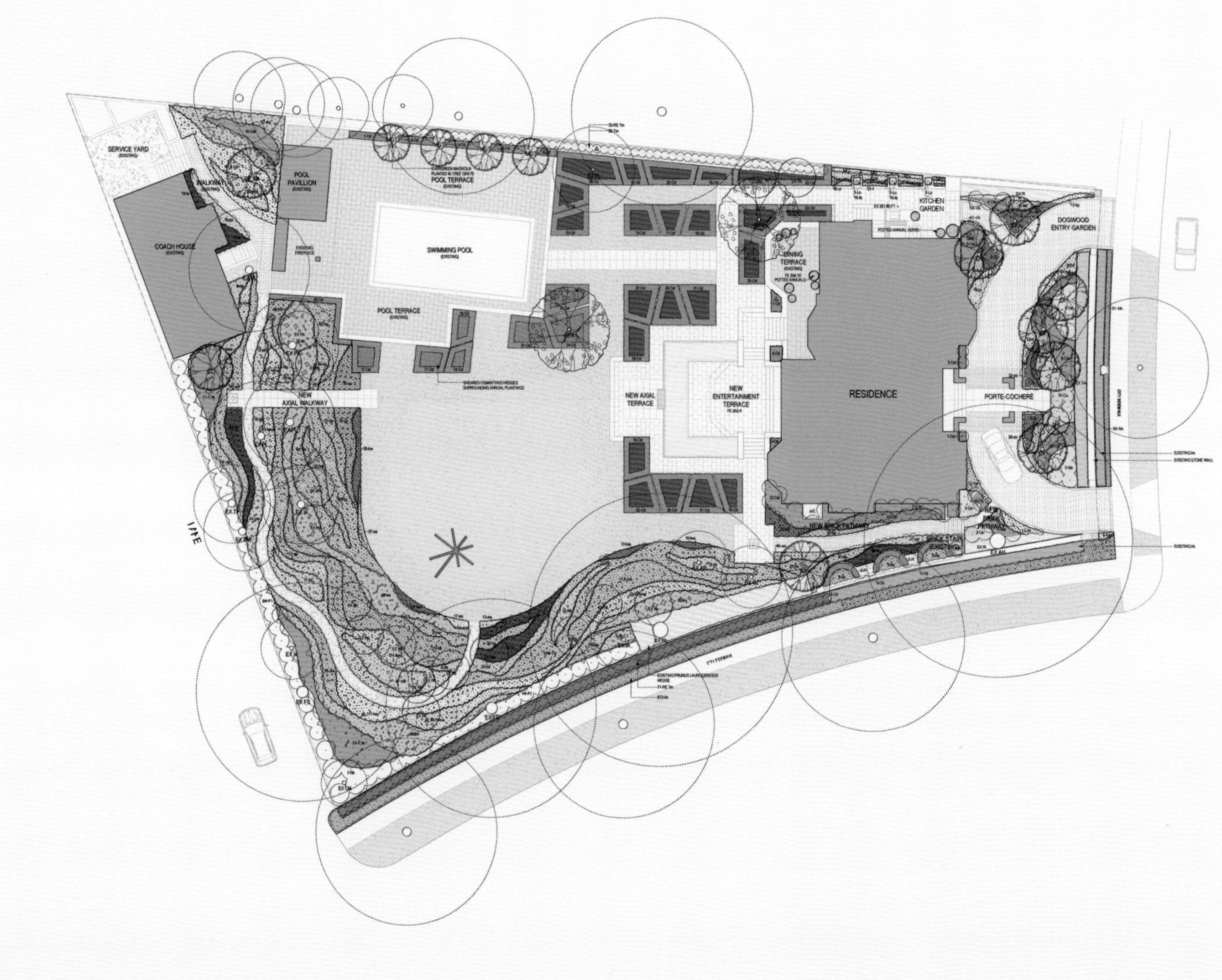

Above. Planting plan.

Right. Folded boxwood parterres link the entertainment and pool terraces.

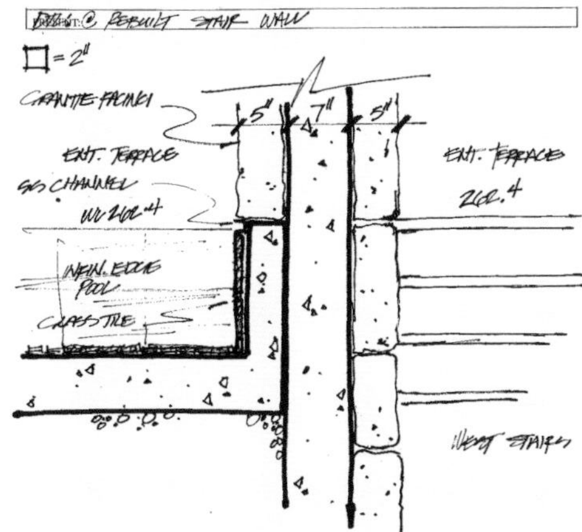

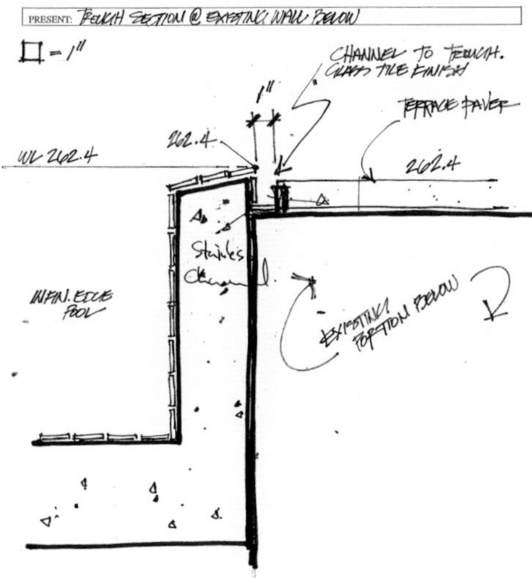

Left. A Gathie Falk dress sculpture on a limestone plinth anchors the reflecting pool.

Above. Conceptual pool details.

Above. The crisp reflective surface of the pool defines the viewing terrace while simultaneously disappearing into the surrounding landscape.

Above and Right. The spring colours of Rhododendrons and Tulips provide a celebration of the season.

Next Spread. The mirrored surface of the reflecting pool acts as a canvas for both the sky and garden, drawing them both into the home's interior.

Right. The sculpture defines the foreground when viewed from the entertainment terrace, while providing an axial anchor for the garden beyond.

Above. The entertainment terrace provides an elevated perspective over the garden that is yeilding a view of the garden's balance of geometric and organic forms.

Above. The Boxwood (*Buxus*) parterres step the elevation down from the residence, entertainment terrace to the lawn.

Next Spread. Folded parterres and brilliant annuals highlight the path to the pool terrace.

Left. Against a backdrop of Rhododendrons, the abstract sculpture juxtaposes colour, texture and geometry.

Right. Boxwood (*Buxus*) parterres lead the eye to the pool terrace.

NO DIVING

Left. A crushed basalt pathway leads from the snowball sculpture, providing an unstructured contrast to the geometry of the central garden space.

Right. Recycled brick paving.

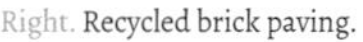

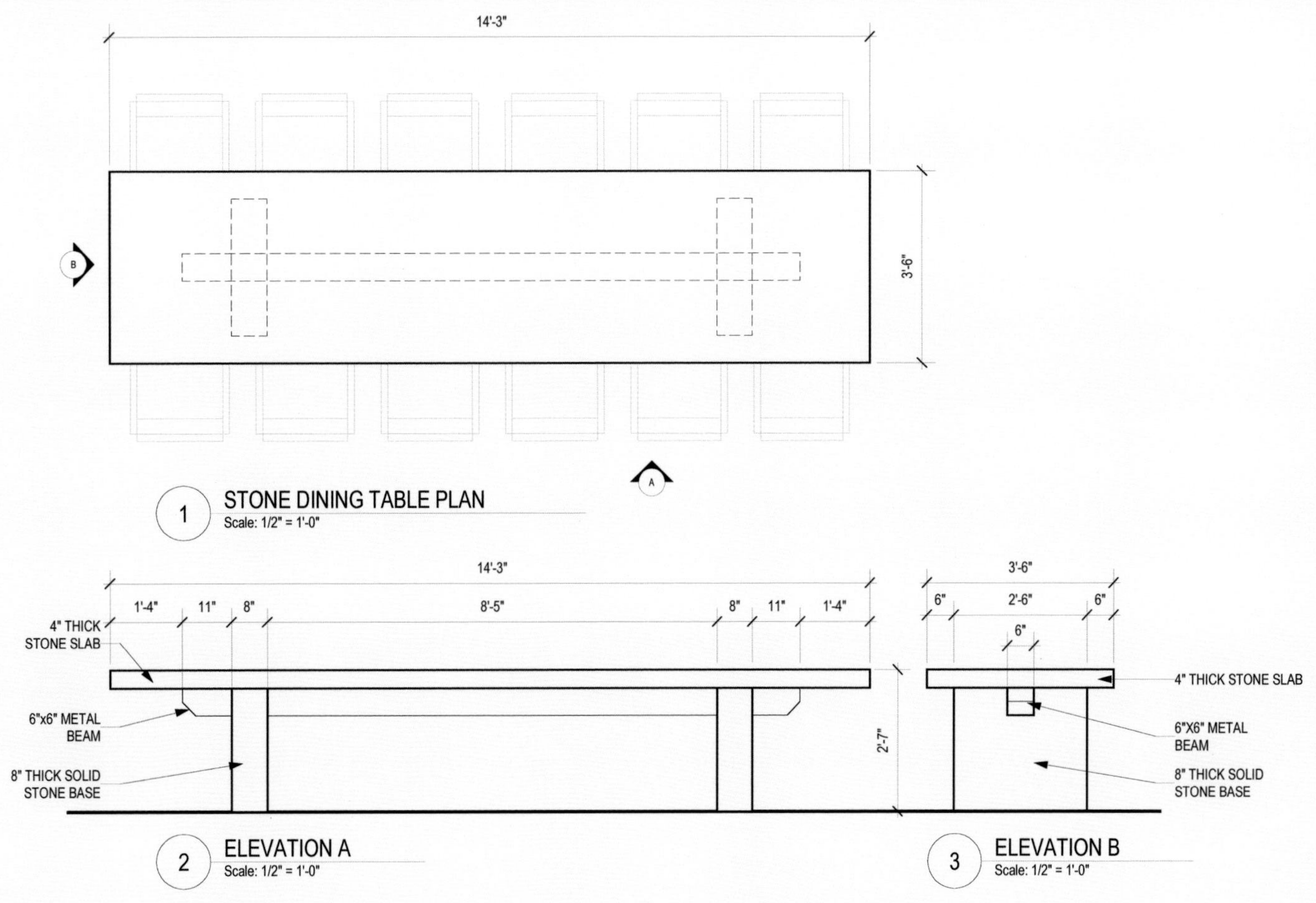

Left. Adjacent to the pool terrace, a stone table and chairs define a space for outdoor dining.

Above. Table details.

Above. Globe Bean Tree (*Catalpa bignoniodes 'Nana'*) and limestone benches define the east edge of the pool terrace.

Right. Solid carved limestone benches and tree trunks invoke a clear rhythm along the east property line.

Next Spread. Twin sculptures frame the view of the garden from the pool house.

7. HILLSIDE JEWEL

Sited on a relatively compact hillside lot, the design of Point Grey challenges the ability of landscape design to expand the space of the house and the landscape. The garden and home are blended together to create a single, seamless unit for living, while maintaining privacy from the street.

Grey Chinese limestone slabs project from the house, at times even starting from inside. This creates backdrops and frames for vegetation like Cutleaf Japanese Maple (*Acer plamatum 'Dissectum'*) and Silver Lace Christmas Rose (*Helleborus argutifolius 'Silver Lace'*). Permutations of the stone planes serve as benches, visual and physical barricades, and ornament. The ephemeral lightness of the planting against the immutable heaviness of the stone results in a sensuous expression throughout the garden. Hedges of Magnolia (*Magnolia grandiflora 'Alta'*) and Yew (*Taxus media 'Hicksii'*) extend the stone walls to define space and to guide movement. Through a careful deployment of gentle slopes and rhythmic stairs, negotiating the topography of the garden feels effortless, as it often does in Sangha's designs.

A turquoise water feature—a water-collecting trough made of recycled glass—is the prominent element in the garden's shady central terrace. The brilliant colour breaks the landscape's muted tones of grey and green, while simultaneously reinforcing its cool colour palette. A serene inlet far away from the tumult of the city, Point Grey is an intimate refuge that breathes a calm expanse into a small-scale site.

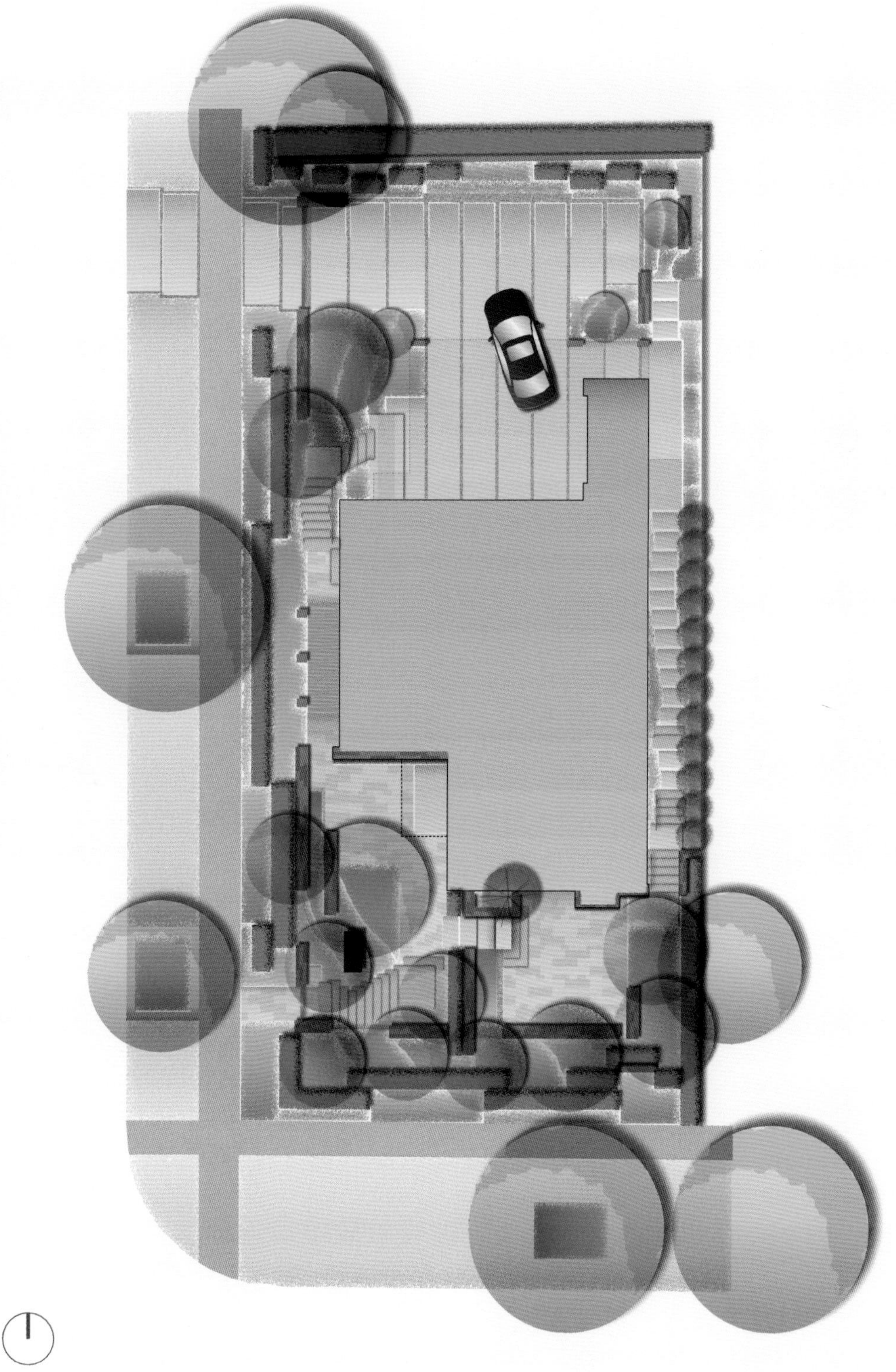

Above. Textural planting and metal picket fencing create a layered foil to the street front.

Right. Evergreen Magnolia (*Magnolia grandiflora*) and Yew (*Taxus*) create layered views of the residence.

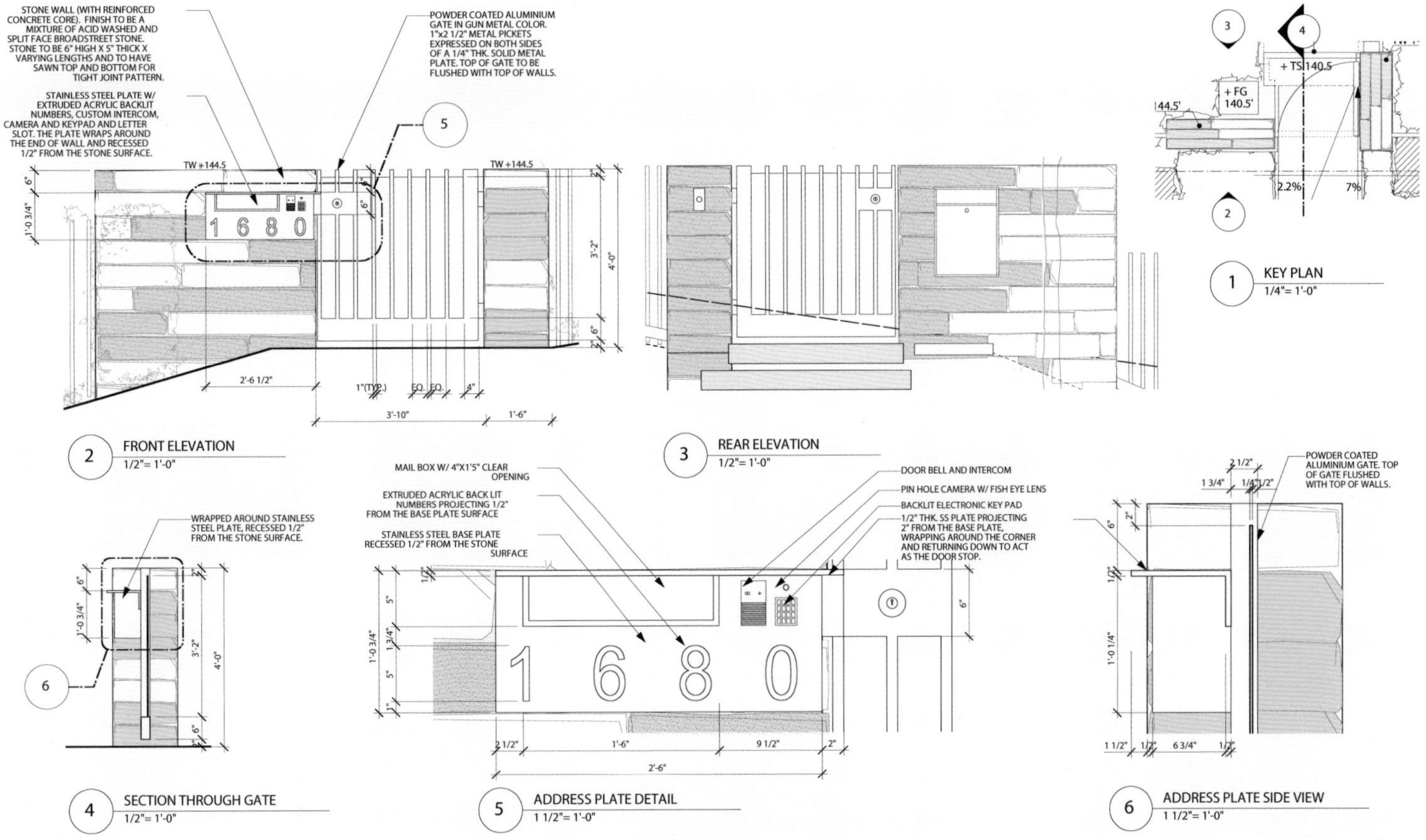

STONE WALL (WITH REINFORCED CONCRETE CORE). FINISH TO BE A MIXTURE OF ACID WASHED AND SPLIT FACE BROADSTREET STONE. STONE TO BE 6" HIGH X 5" THICK X VARYING LENGTHS AND TO HAVE SAWN TOP AND BOTTOM FOR TIGHT JOINT PATTERN.

STAINLESS STEEL PLATE W/ EXTRUDED ACRYLIC BACKLIT NUMBERS, CUSTOM INTERCOM, CAMERA AND KEYPAD AND LETTER SLOT. THE PLATE WRAPS AROUND THE END OF WALL AND RECESSED 1/2" FROM THE STONE SURFACE.

POWDER COATED ALUMINIUM GATE IN GUN METAL COLOR. 1"x2 1/2" METAL PICKETS EXPRESSED ON BOTH SIDES OF A 1/4" THK. SOLID METAL PLATE. TOP OF GATE TO BE FLUSHED WITH TOP OF WALLS.

TW +144.5

1 6 8 0

2 FRONT ELEVATION
1/2"= 1'-0"

3 REAR ELEVATION
1/2"= 1'-0"

+ TS 140.5

+ FG 140.5'

144.5'

2.2%

7%

1 KEY PLAN
1/4"= 1'-0"

WRAPPED AROUND STAINLESS STEEL PLATE, RECESSED 1/2" FROM THE STONE SURFACE.

4 SECTION THROUGH GATE
1/2"= 1'-0"

MAIL BOX W/ 4"X1'5" CLEAR OPENING

EXTRUDED ACRYLIC BACK LIT NUMBERS PROJECTING 1/2" FROM THE BASE PLATE SURFACE

STAINLESS STEEL BASE PLATE RECESSED 1/2" FROM THE STONE SURFACE

DOOR BELL AND INTERCOM

PIN HOLE CAMERA W/ FISH EYE LENS

BACKLIT ELECTRONIC KEY PAD

1/2" THK. SS PLATE PROJECTING 2" FROM THE BASE PLATE, WRAPPING AROUND THE CORNER AND RETURNING DOWN TO ACT AS THE DOOR STOP.

1 6 8 0

5 ADDRESS PLATE DETAIL
1 1/2"= 1'-0"

POWDER COATED ALUMINIUM GATE. TOP OF GATE FLUSHED WITH TOP OF WALLS.

6 ADDRESS PLATE SIDE VIEW
1 1/2"= 1'-0"

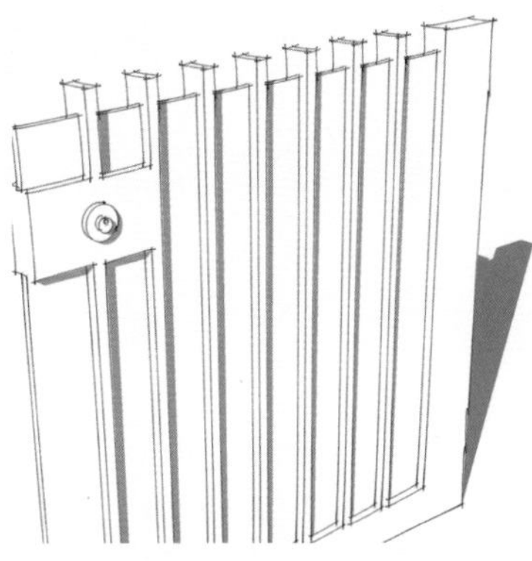

Left and Right. Vertical metal pickets on the autocourt gate and pedestrian gate contrast with the horizontal lines of the adjacent limestone.

Above. Limestone stairs float through a verdant landscape.

Above. The entry stairs wind around a pivotal bronze sculpture to the entry courtyard.

Left. The side yard glistens after a spring rain.

Right. 3D models and garden elevations.

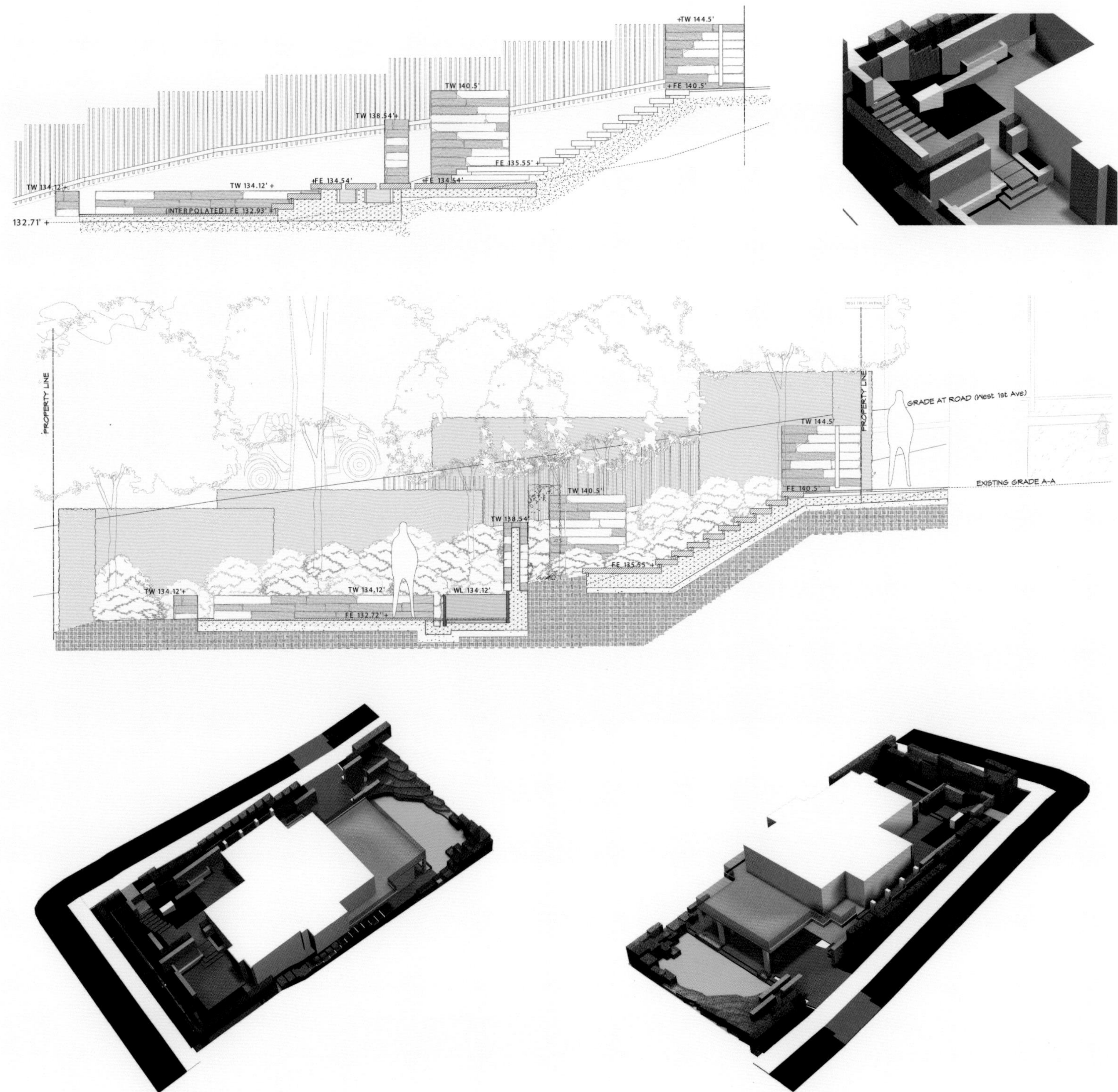
TW 144.5'
TW 140.5'
FE 140.5'
TW 138.54'
FE 135.55'
TW 134.12'
FE 134.54'
TW 134.12'
FE 134.54'
(INTERPOLATED) FE 132.93'
132.71'
PROPERTY LINE
GRADE AT ROAD (West 1st Ave)
TW 144.5'
PROPERTY LINE
EXISTING GRADE A-A
TW 140.5'
FE 140.5'
TW 138.54'
FE 135.55'
TW 134.12'
TW 134.12'
WL 134.12'
FE 132.72'

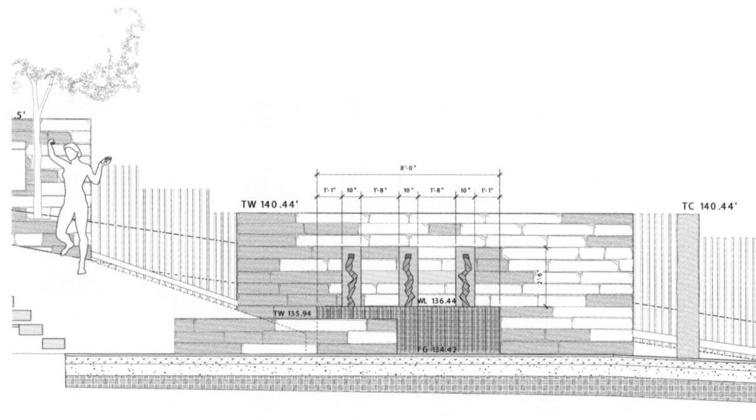

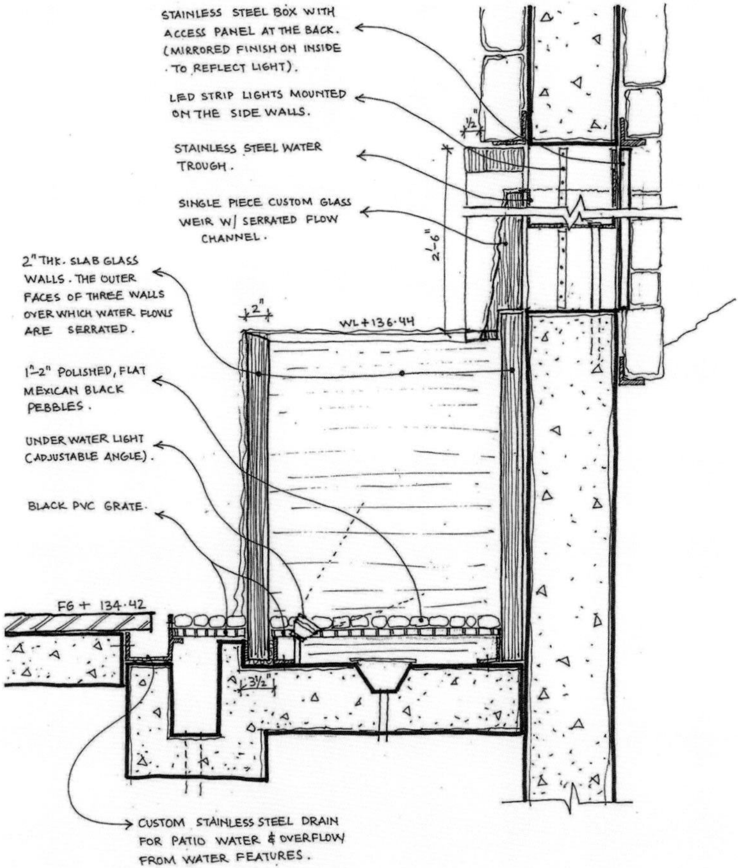

Above. Water feature details.

Right. A sculptural recycled glass water feature is inset into the textured limestone wall, anchoring the entry courtyard.

Above. Glass, stone and plantings frame a vignette of the entry courtyard.

Right. Interlinked rectilinear volumes and consistency of materials unite landscape and residence on the south side of the meditation courtyard. Black Bamboo (*Phyllostachys nigra*) adds lightness and movement to the roof garden.

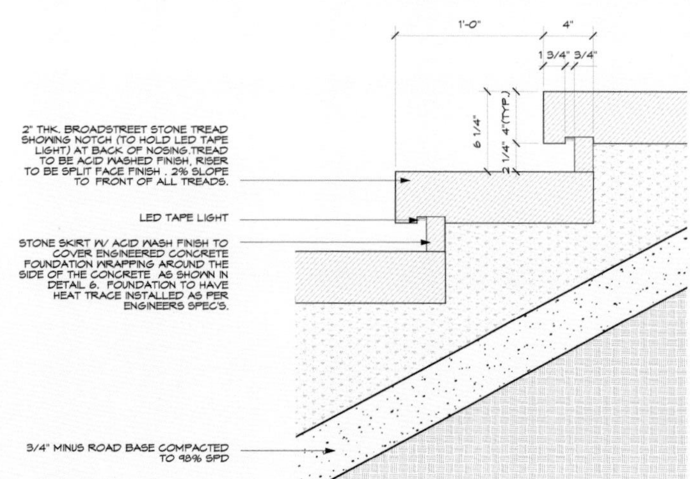

Left. Limestone stair detail.

Right. Subtle shifts of texture within a minimal hardscape palette create a sense of calm at every scale.

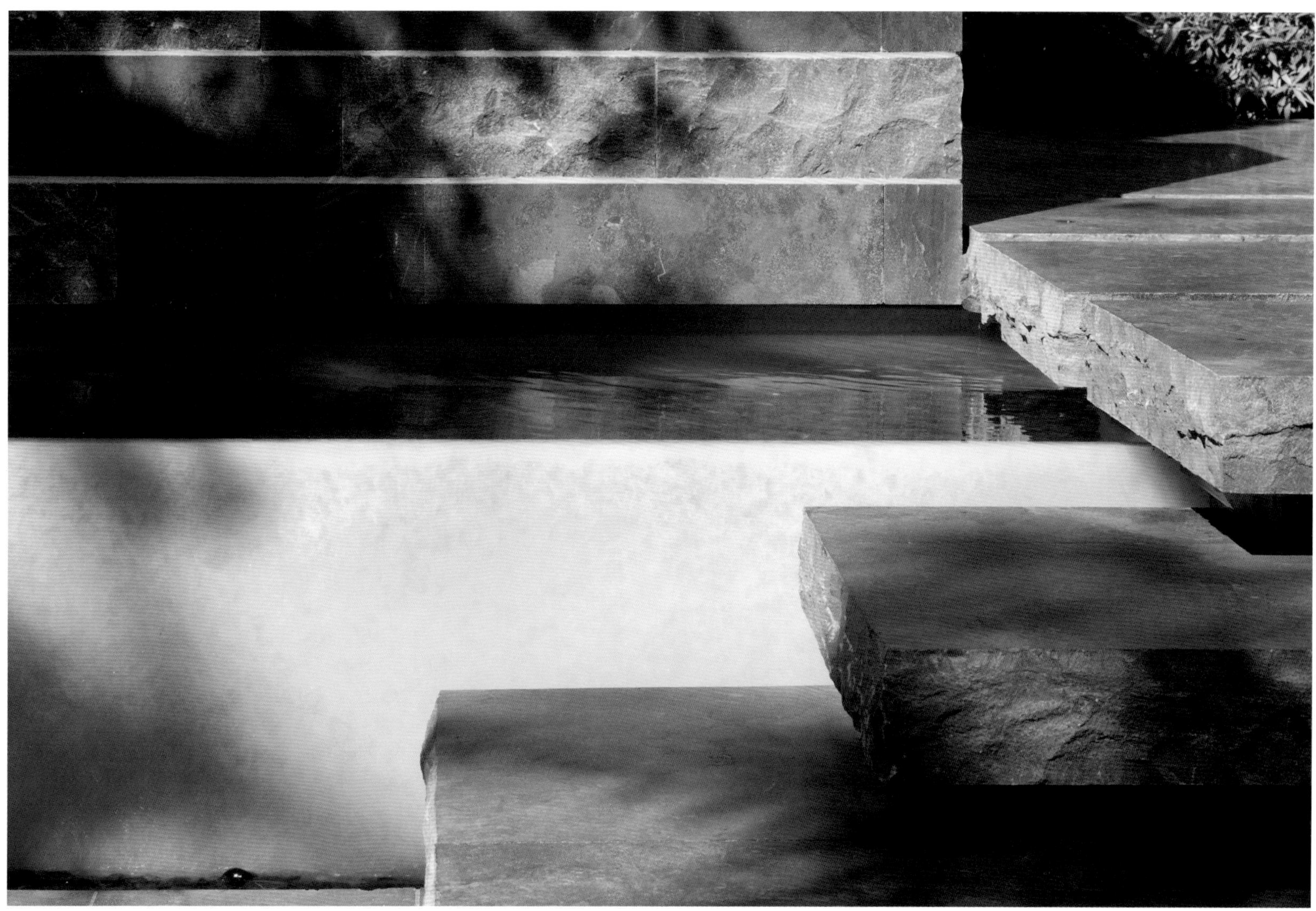

Left and Above. Crafted by a local glass artisan, the garden's sculptural recycled glass elements reference the luminous colour of glacier-fed pools.

Left, Right and Next Spread. Attention to detail, lighting and textural planting highlight the rhythmic quality of the garden.

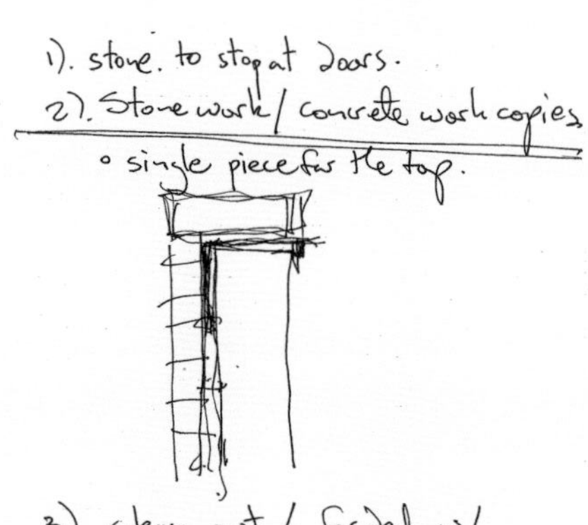

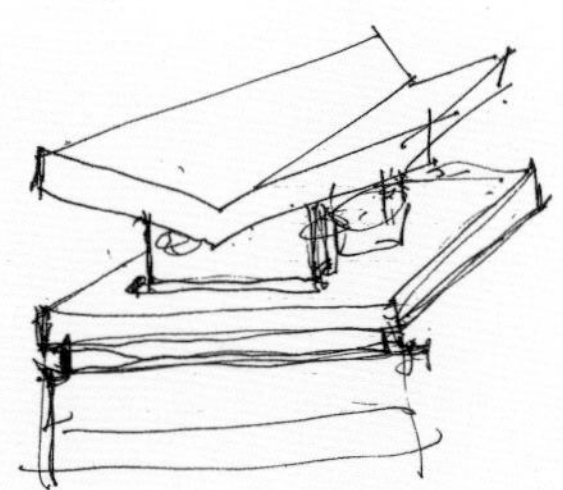

Above. Garden gives way to the powerful city and mountain views.

Below Left. Fireplace cap sketch.

Right. A fireplace and lighting add a warm glow to the roof terrace, while bamboo provides privacy.

Left. The textured foliage of Black Bamboo (*Phyllostachys Nigra*), ferns, Hemlock *(Tsuga)* and the warm tones of Ipe wood fencing create an intimate and inviting passage from the autocourt into the meditation terrace.

Right. Solid limestone columns visually extend the foreground wall, framing the views of the planting along the west walkway.

BEFORE & AFTER

8. QUINTESSENTIAL

A steeply graded driveway dips down from the street to the *porte-cocherè*, which is bounded by a striking water feature. Made by a local artist from an impressively large piece of emerald green jade, a sculpture appears to float on the top of the surface of a slate blue pool. The weathered Corten steel wall behind the work is a multifaceted volume that conjures the coastal mountains of British Columbia. Between the mountains, water pours like snow melt down a stainless steel water course. The bold gesture of the feature near the main entry door is an enticing invitation into the space and a harbinger of the wondrous landscape to come.

Quintessential is a moving picture of a landscape: with seemingly every step is a new reveal and an enriched understanding of what the garden is and what it possesses. From the entry garden, a grove of Mountain Hemlock (*Tsuga mertensiana*) leads around the side of the house to a small terrace with a table also made of jade, imparting a sense of material continuity. Extending from the living room, a large terrace affords views of another terrace below and of a lawn shaped like a leaf blade. Past the sculpted lawn, a vast view of a ravine with old growth forest opens up. A much larger lawn meets a pavilion that overlooks the ravine. The meeting of the built environment and the forest is surreal, and the pavilion allows one to soak in the confluence.

A koi pond consisting of multiple pools treats the ears to a pleasant babble as the water circulates. An artist was commissioned to carefully place columns of local basalt to achieve the best spatial and acoustic effects. Above the pond is a large sculpture of a Beech leaf, made from local jade, standing as if dropped from a tree and celebrating the Beech trees on the property. Nearby is another pavilion, this one offering a full view of almost the entire designed landscape. Here one can bear witness to the beautifully spun web of axes and paths that crisscross the property, visually connecting garden elements and creating an evocative narrative for the site.

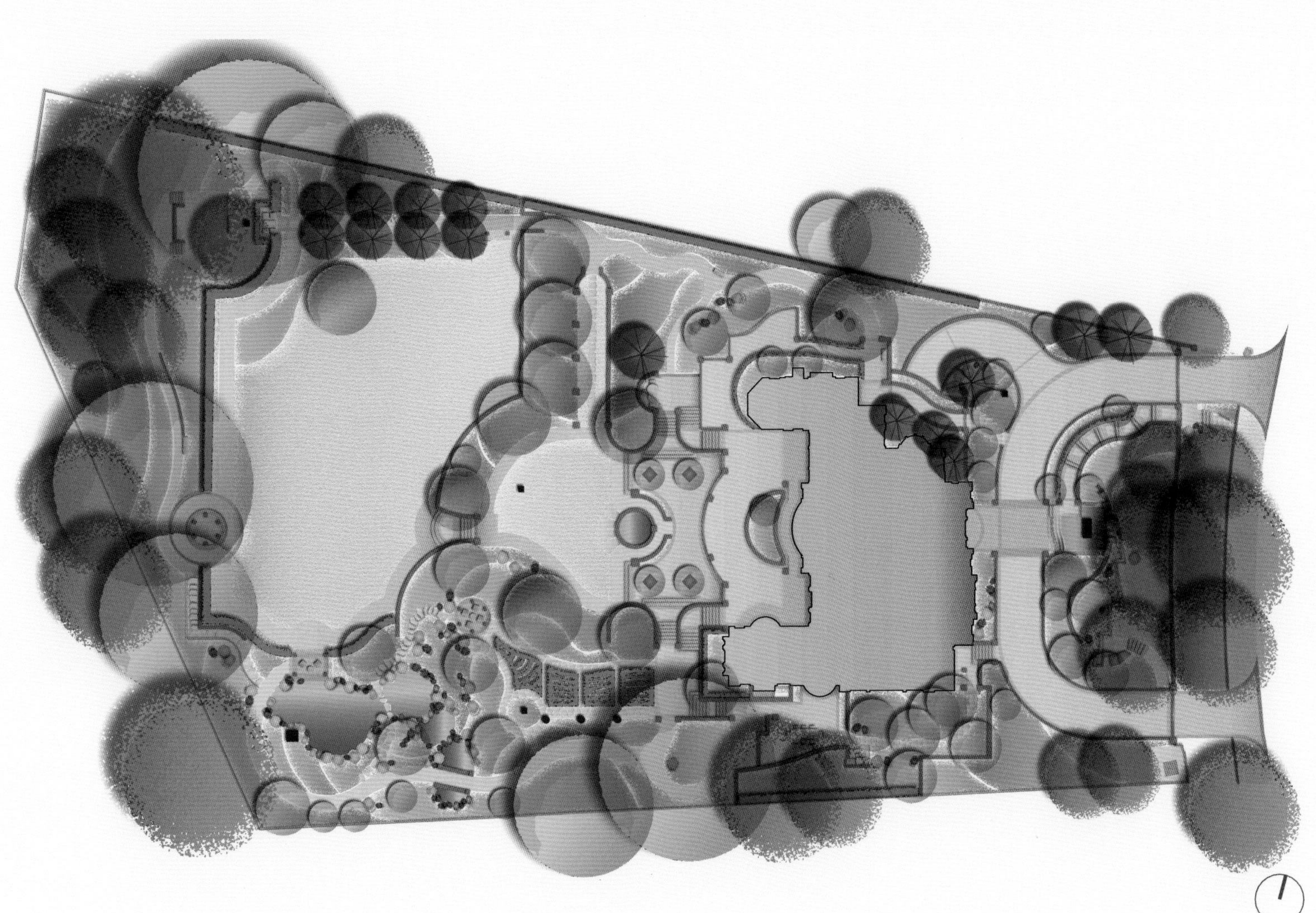

Left. Begonia and Boxwood (*Buxus*) along the entry walk echo the soft curve of the entry drive. The loose canopy of Japanese Maple (*Acer palmatum 'Artropurpureum'*) over the entry stairs provides refuge for the pedestrian path.

Above. The port cochere provides shelter and frames views to the garden.

Left and Right. The entry court reflecting pool unites a George Pratt jade sculpture and articulated Corten steel, anchoring the axial view from the front door.

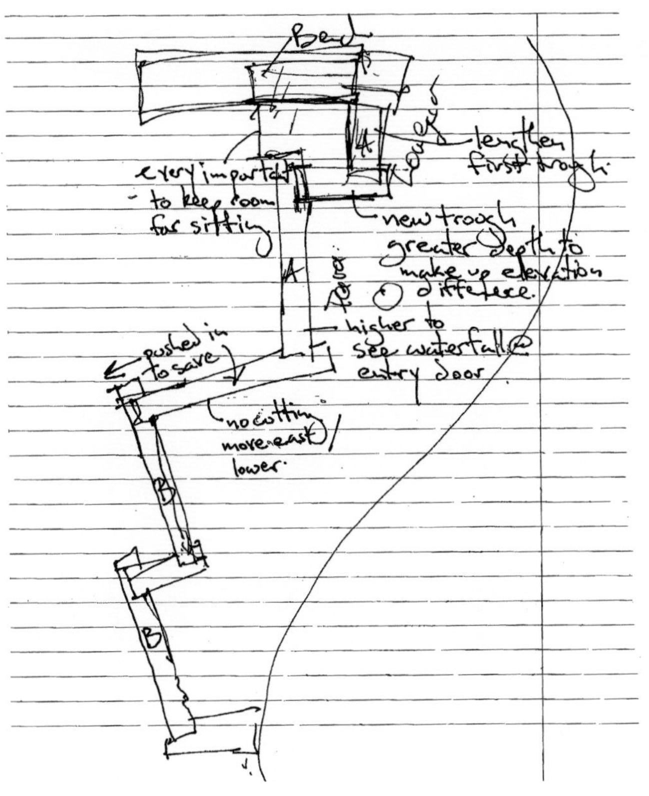
Bench
lower
lengthen first trough
every important - to keep room for sitting
new trough greater depth to make up elevation difference
higher to see waterfall @ entry door
pushed in to save
no cutting move east lower
A
B
B

Above. Planting Concept Development.

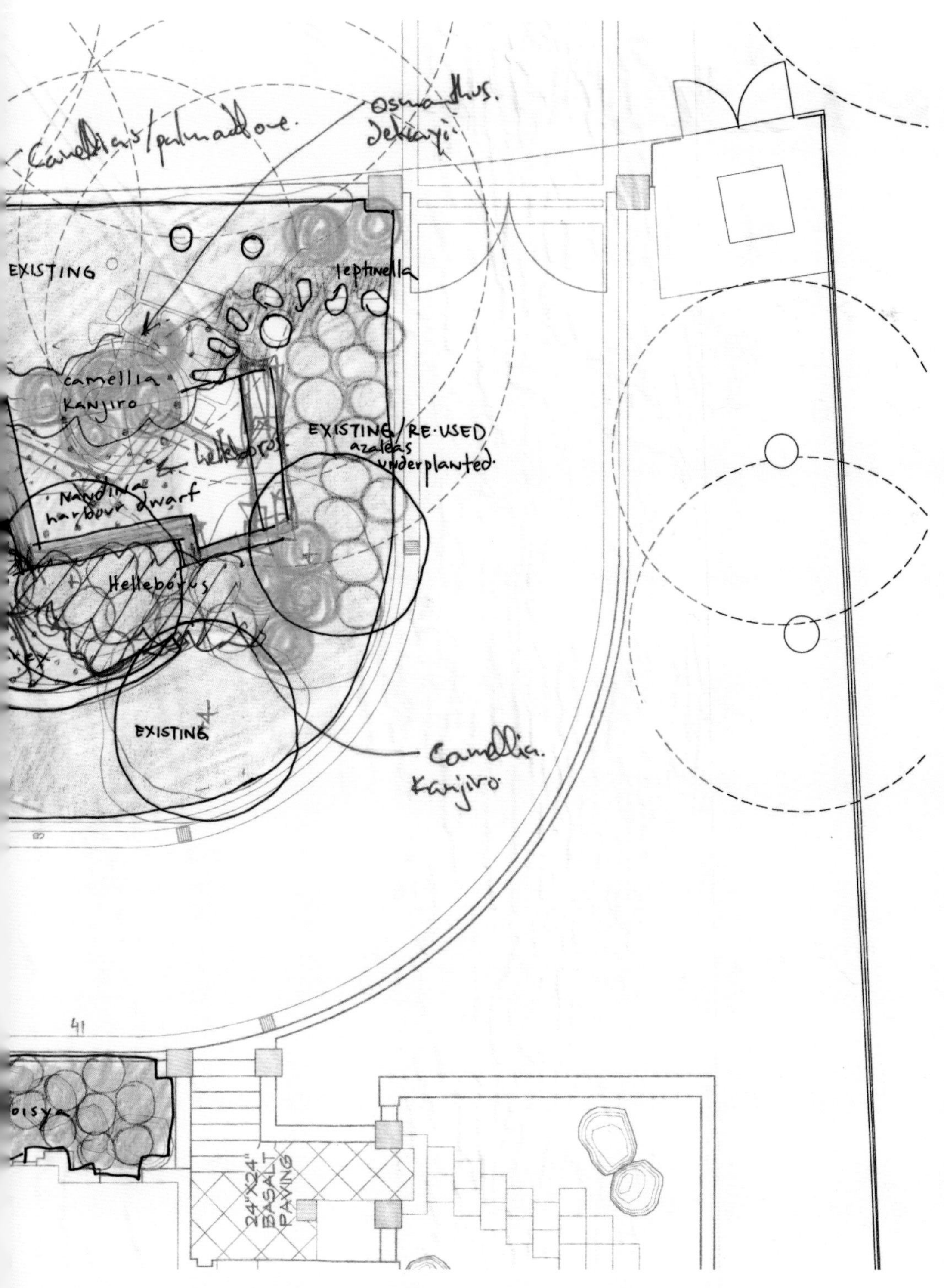
Osmanthus. Delavayi
EXISTING
leptinella
camellia Kanjiro
EXISTING/RE·USED
azaleas underplanted.
Nandina harbour dwarf
Helleborus
EXISTING
Camellia. Kanjiro
24"X24" BASALT PAVING

Previous Spread. Neoclassical retaining walls both define space and provide a canvas for the peeling bark of Paperbark Maple (*Acer griseum*).

Above. Pattern and form allow for rich visual experiences from all aspects of the garden.

Above. Sculptural planters provide an architectural backdrop for the pattern garden and a formal link to the pavilion nestled in the trees.

Right. Dappled light plays on the cinnamon bark of Paperbark Maples (*Acer griseum*) and textural planting.

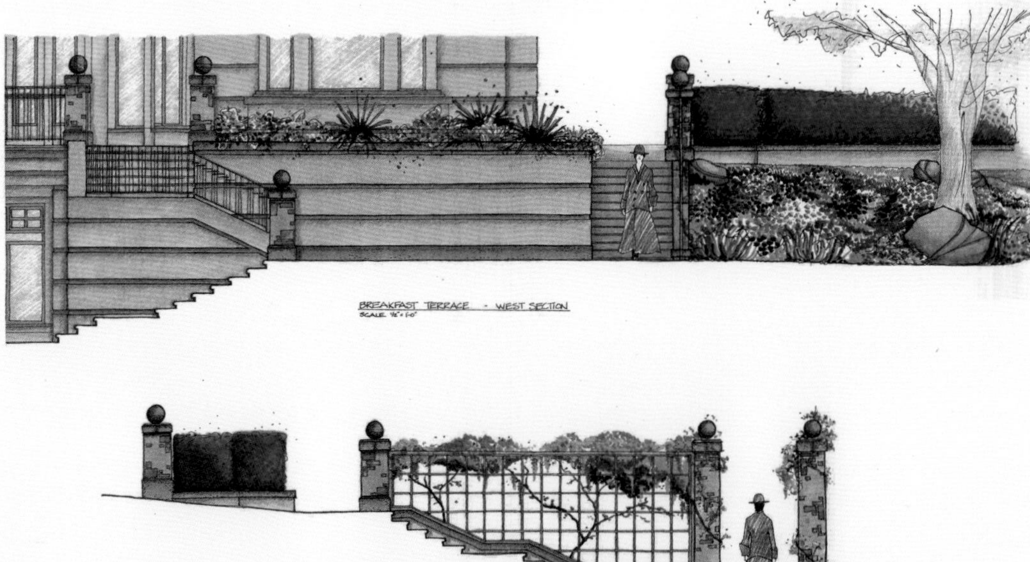

Above. Entry, retaining wall and conceptual drawings.

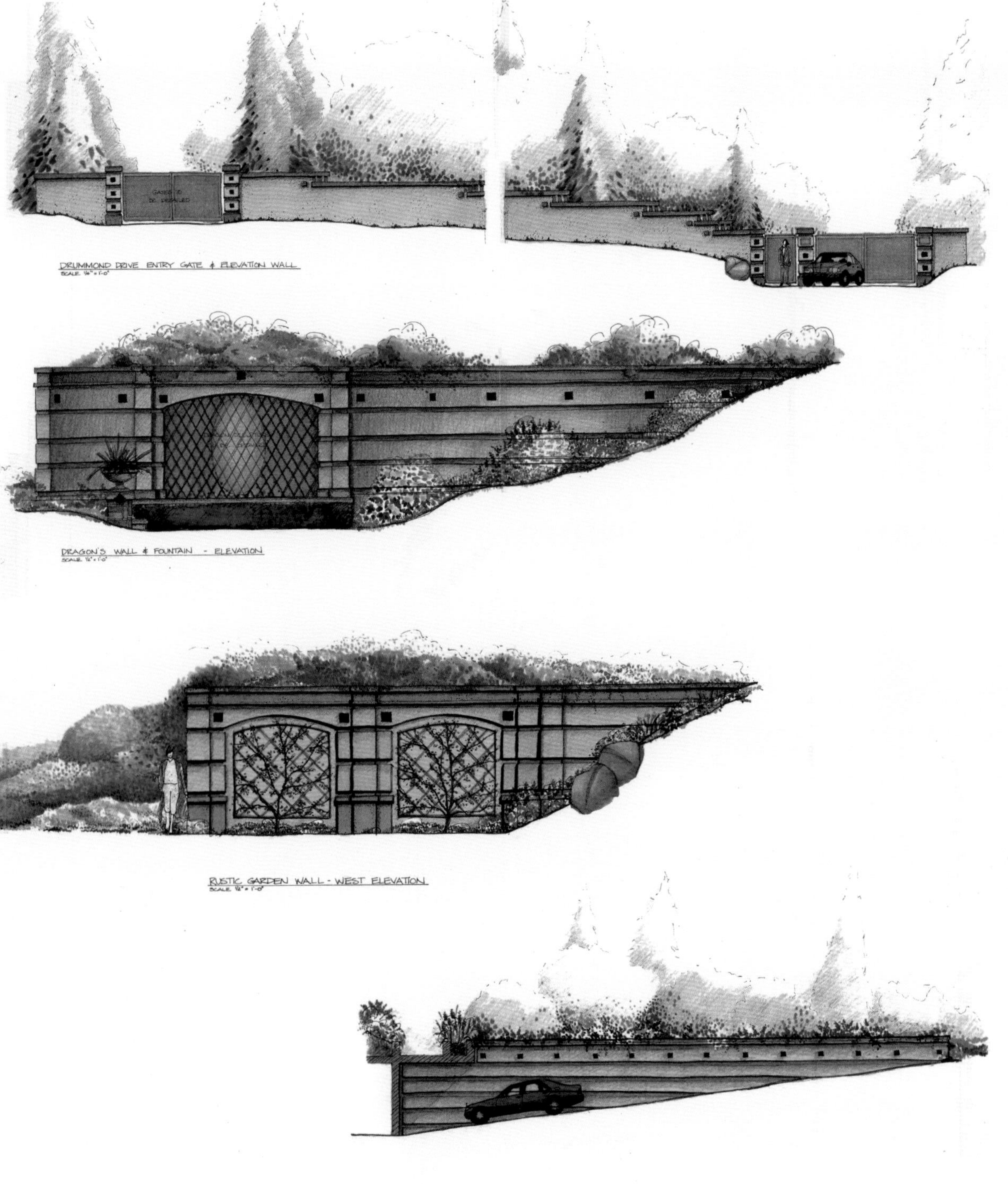

AUTO RAMP WALL - ELEVATION
SCALE 1/4" = 1'-0"

Above. The vibrant colours of new bulbs and fresh leaves, herald the arrival of spring.

Right . Sculptural planters provide an architectural backdrop for the pattern garden.

Above and Right. Layers of spring colour, texture and form blanket the annual display beds and planters.

Left. A sculptural organic-shaped Jade table provides a foil for the neoclassical architecture.

Right. White azaleas enliven the view from the den window.

Next Spread. Brilliant annuals drape the sloped curves of the display garden.

Above. Spring bulbs provide a brilliant display to the fountain terrace.

Right. Brilliant annuals link custom precast pots with the display garden.

Above. Fluid channels of blooms draw the eye between spaces and reinforce the sinuous forms of the adjacent path.

Right. The fountain terrace is a neoclassical balance of architectural form, colour and texture.

Next Spread. The garden design balances and accentuates the property's architecture through its subtle expression of neoclassical form and expression of calm tranquility.

Above. A layered view provides an intriguing vignette of colour and form.

Right. A gurgling fountain enlivens the pool terrace and anchors the central garden axis.

Left. As a play between neoclassical formality and contemporary asymmetry, the lawn reinforces and juxtaposes the axis between the residence and ravine.

Right. Elevations and details.

GARDEN WALK - SOUTH ELEVATION
SCALE 1/2" = 1'-0"

FOUNTAIN - WEST ELEVATION
SCALE 1/2" = 1'-0"

GARDEN POT ON PEDESTAL
SCALE 1" = 1'-0"

STAIRS TO GREAT LAWN - WEST ELEVATION
SCALE 1/2" = 1'-0"

Above. Japanese Maples (*Acer palmatum*) canopy basalt stones and the Koi pond.

Right. Stone waterfalls flow between pools leading to the Koi pond. Moss, and Moon-Leaf Japanese Maple (*Acer japonicum*) drape over the channel.

Above. Sculptural basalt boulders puncture through verdant green groundcover.

Left. Stepping stones and sculptural railings define a meandering pathway.

Left. Yellow canes of Black Bamboo (*Phyllostachys nigra*) puncture through a mass of Sweet Box (*Sarcococca*) behind a sculptural branch rail by Mike Maca.

Right. Sculptural metal grab rails and stone intertwine along the Koi pond pathway.

Left. The ravine pavilion terminates the central garden axis and provides an inviting vantage point over the ravine.

Above. A stone wall defines the edge of the lawn and the lush planting above.

Above. Variations in colour and texture give depth to the planted border and hint at a landscape beyond.

Left and Above. Located on the pivotal knoll in the garden, the jewel pavilion is an ideal viewing point for the Koi ponds, pattern garden and lawn terraces.

Above. The ravine and White Pines (*Pinus strobus 'Fastigiata'*) provide a backdrop to the spring colours of Rhododendrons and an existing Golden Chain (*Laburnum*) anchoring the lawn terrace.

Above. A winding walkway through the Rhododendrons leads to the allée pavilion.

Left and Right. Framed by the columns of the gateway pavilion, a Matt Devine sculpture is both pivotal and invites the eye into the Koi pond garden.

Left. Anchored by pavilions on both ends, the Pine (*Pinus strobus 'Fastigiata'*) allée frames views to the ravine beyond.

Right. Pavilion and overview details.

Next Spread. The ravine pavilion holds the boundary between the neoclassical garden and the ravine beyond.

GATEWAY PAVILION - EAST ELEVATION
SCALE 1" = 1'-0"

GATEWAY PAVILION - NORTH ELEVATION
SCALE 1" = 1'-0"

OVERVIEW PAVILION - WEST ELEVATION
SCALE 1" = 1'-0"

OVERVIEW PAVILION - NORTH ELEVATION
SCALE 1" = 1'-0"

OVERVIEW PAVILION - PLAN
SCALE 1/8" = 1'-0"

OVERVIEW - EAST ELEVATION
SCALE 1/2" = 1'-0"

Left. Canopied by Copper Beech Trees (*Fagus sylvatica*), the ravine pavilion provides a quiet vantage point to the forest beyond.

Above. Pavilion details.

Above. Flagstone walkways wind through the ravine forest canopy.

EVOLUTION

9. TEXTURES

Textures highlights landscape architecture as a living artistic medium. Expressive, bold, and geometrically pleasing, the project is a balanced composition of rectilinear forms and expressive planting. Textures embraces a contemporary house chiefly composed of glass, allowing the landscape to animate the inside of the home, as well as the home to animate the landscape. Sightlines between the contemporary art collection inside and the abstract sculptural works outside strengthen the bond between home and grounds. Through an economy of means and sensitivity to natural materials, the design delivers a stirring, sensuous landscape.

Viewed from the street, a stand of old growth Douglas Fir (*Pseudotsuga*) trees conceals the garden. Making a right angle near the property edge, a path with a steady, even tempo passes from the pedestrian gate through plantings of varying tactile qualities — the soft, fragile flowers of Lenten Rose (Helleborus orientalis), the springy spikes of Foam Flowers (*Tiarella 'Spring Symphony'*) and the rigid leaves of Yucca (*Yucca filamentosa*)—immersing the user in a sea of textures. The path leads to an open lawn and a set of resplendent onyx pools. The upper pool bounds the back of the house as a reflection pool, while the lower pool is used for swimming.

Up a small set of stairs and past the dining terrace, a square garden with an off-centered Southern Magnolia (*Magnolia grandiflora*) aligns with a hot tub. Around the other side of the house, the path picks up again, wandering through another absorbing array of plants chosen for their texture. It continues past a garden of Japanese Timber Bamboo (*Phyllostachys bambusoides*) planted in a below-grade lightwell and stretching nearly as high as the two storey home.

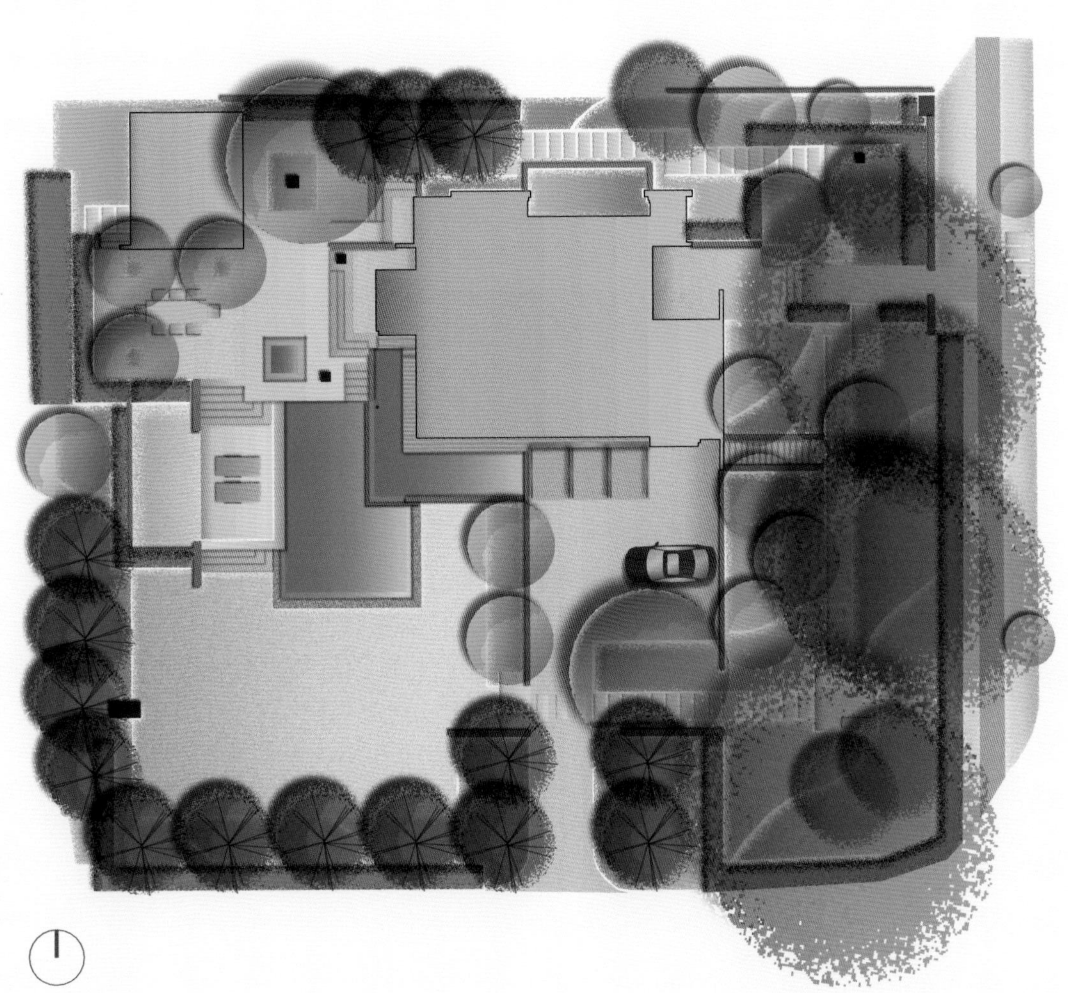

Left and Right. Light plays on an etched glass and metal entry gate, welcoming visitors as they pass through the stand of mature Fir (*Pseudotsuga*) and Cedar (*Thuja*) on their way to the residence.

6287

Left. Textural architectural planting creates an understorey to the existing Cedar (*Thuja*) and Fir (*Abies*) trees.

Right. Viewing the entry from the bench, expressive plantings provide a textural layer between the architecture and hardscap.

Above. A Buddha collected during the client's travels is enveloped in exuberant planting and dappled light.

Right. At the end of a concrete walkway an offset concrete bench alludes to a landscape beyond.

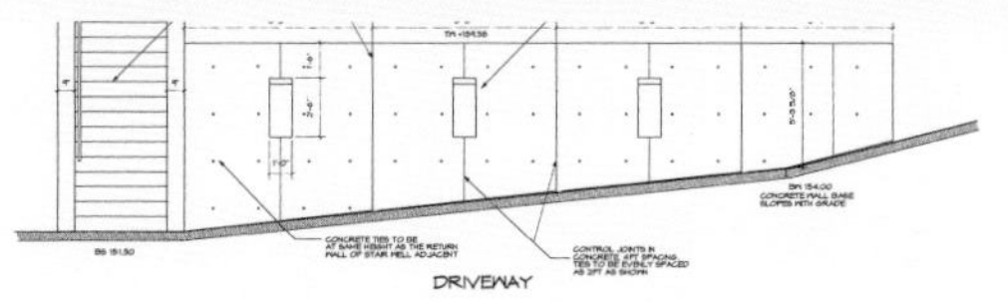

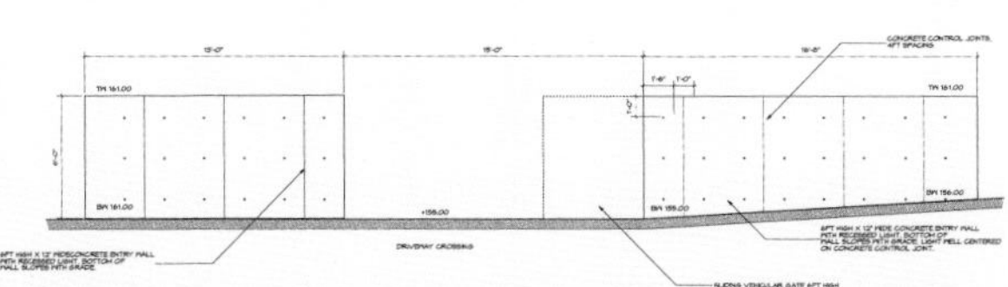

Left. A bold cantilevered wing projects over a lower retaining wall in the autocourt. A pedestrian access slides below while reveals and lighting niches create rhythm and interest.

Above Right. Retaining wall detail.

Right. Frosted glass and metal autocourt gate.

Left and Above. Sliding glass curtain doors and consistent layout of indoor and outdoor flooring emphasize the interconectivity of the interior and exterior worlds.

Next Spread. The terraced pools and patios provide a transition between building and landscape.

Above. Attention to every detail is reflected in the care given to defining reveals, materials and transitions.

Left. Sculptural concrete walls and stairs connect the pool and lawn terraces.

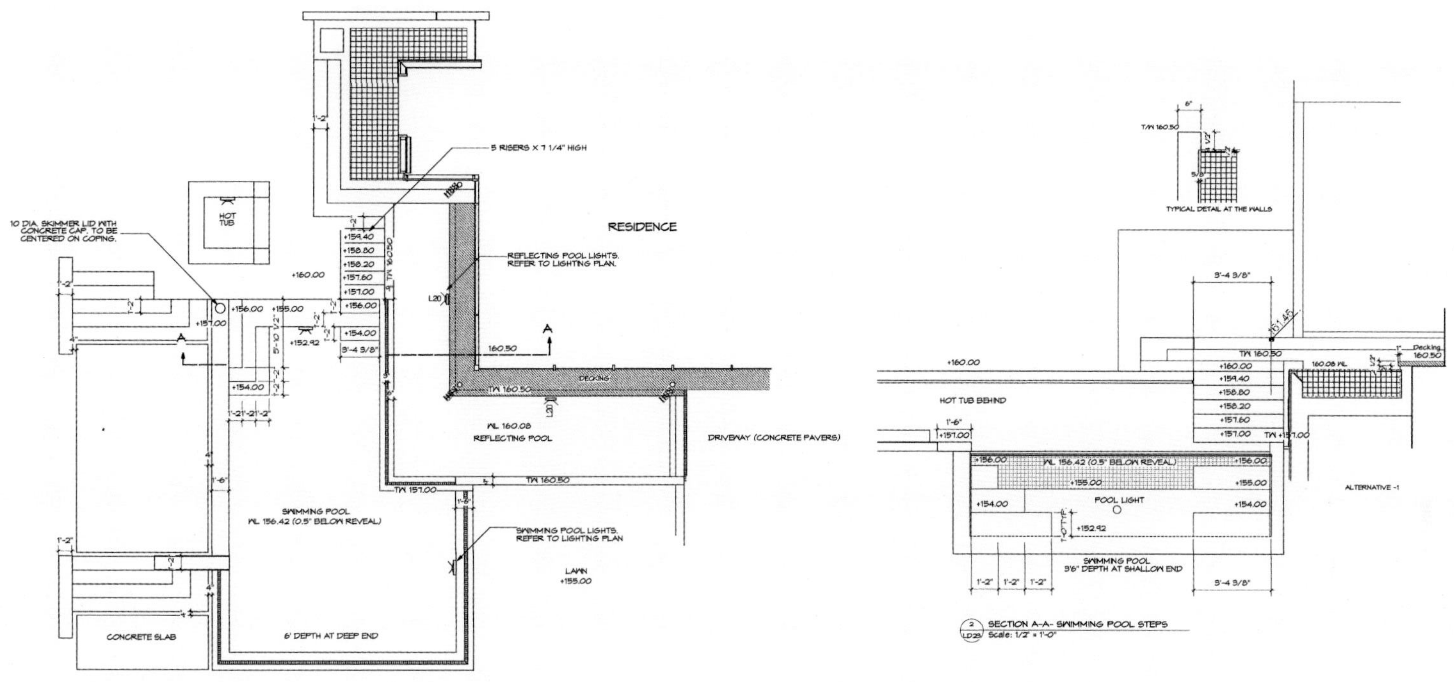

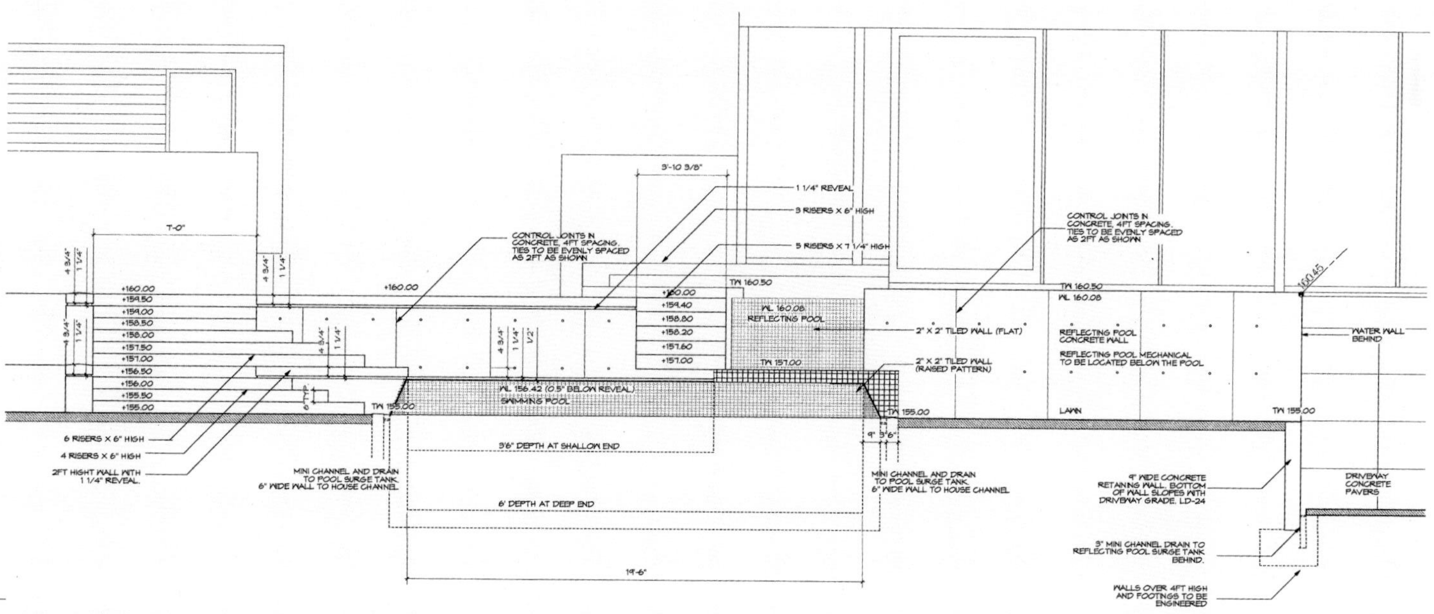

Above. Pool terrace details

Left and Above. The raised concrete pool walls lead the eye to its visual terminus at the lower pool and reinforce the depth of field.

Above Left. Acting as a sculptural plinth for the residence, the dark tiled reflecting pool draws in a larger landscape of sky and vegetation.

Left. A sculptural chaise provides an organic counterpoint to the geometric forms of the pools and terraces.

Right. The surface of the pool is made luminous when pattern and reflection merge.

Above. Architectural concrete walls, sculpture and trees are reflected in the mirror surface of the pool.

Left. Invisible edge pools provide a visual transition between residence and landscape.

Above. Bold textural contrast and forms create drama in the evening light.

Right. A large iron urn focuses views and provides a terminus for the axial garden path.

Above. Architectural and landscape forms merge and blur the lines between the two.

Left. The shade under a bosque of Persian Ironwood (*Parrotia persica*) provides a sheltered prospect from which to enjoy views of the residence.

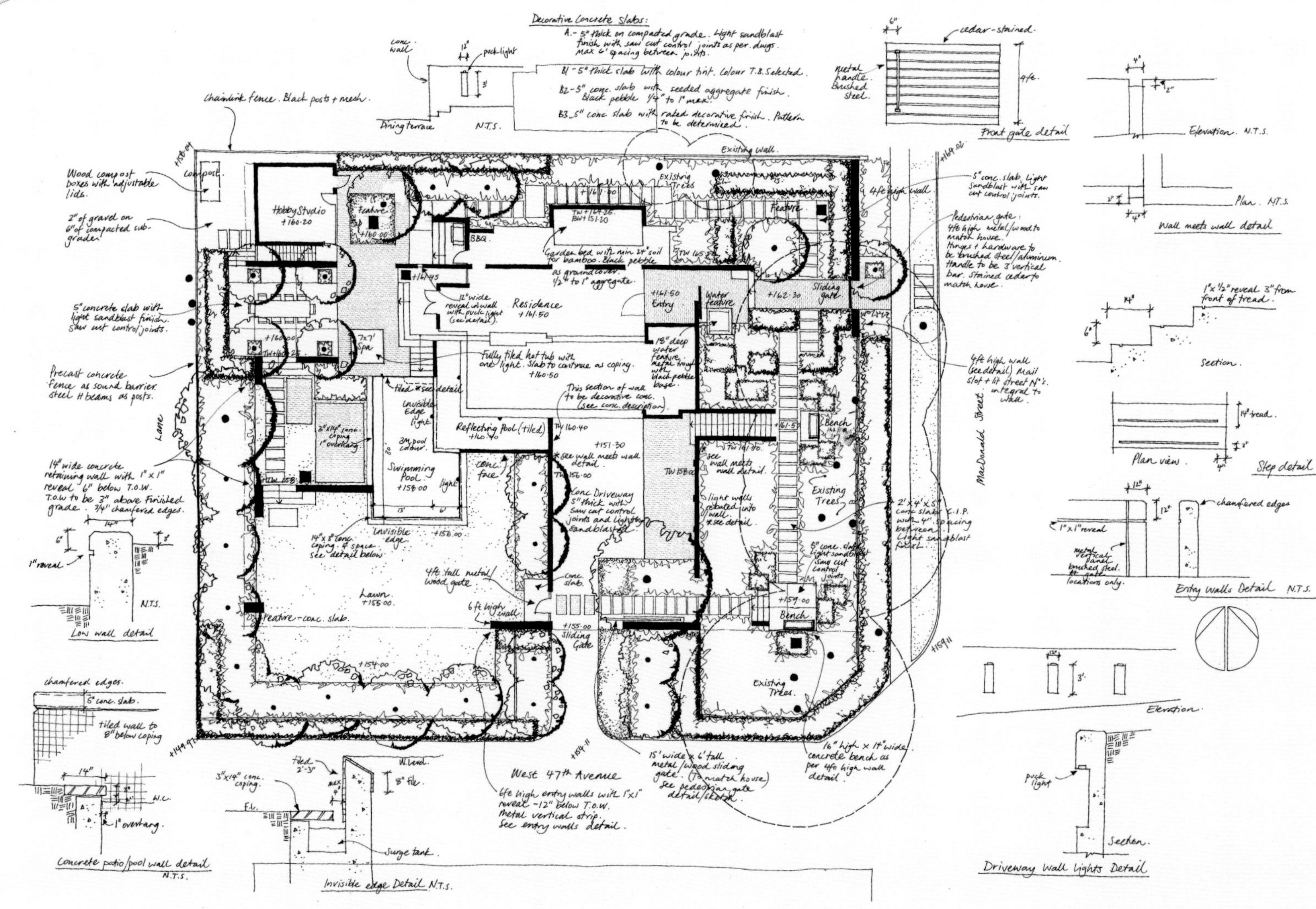

Above. Landscape plan and conceptual details.

Right. A framed view to the west features the dining terrace below the Persian Ironwood (*Parrotia persica*) and sculptural stairs spilling down to the pool terrace.

Left and Above. Dark during the day, the pools become beacons of light in the evening

Next Spread. Reflections of garden and home unite in the pools as dusk sets.

CONSTRUCTION & COMPLETION

CRAFTING

10. OUTLOOK

Drawing on the aesthetic of a French garden, Outlook is an evolving narrative of layers, transitions, and grand reveals. An auto court weaves through mature Beech, White Oak, and Himalayan Cedar to reach the entrance of the house, which is sited strategically on the corner of the property to preserve the landscape. Walking through the garden, a vast mountain view blossoms from a succession of enclosed spaces. Past a veil of crab apple trees, a series of sweeping oval lawns cascade down the hillside. The view, the garden, and the house feel in synchronization and in balance with one another, with neither element taking more attention than another.

Outlook is a playground for the senses: colour operates as a space maker, smell intoxicates thoughts, and sounds make blissful music. Outside the library, a pattern garden reaches from the house to a basketball court. Arranged by colour gradient—warmer colours closer to the house, cooler colours further away—the plants set the area ablaze and visually expand the interstitial space. Planted according to the colour wheel, a colour garden marks the last oval lawn in the landscape.

Along a walkway that frames the east side of the oval lawns, a scent garden engulfs the senses, evoking memories, feelings, and dreams. Along the west side, vegetable gardens offer a tactile repose. Spilling down from the northeast garden terraces, waterfalls empty out into a Koi pond where a wood deck provides refuge for the fish, as well as a perch from which to absorb the hushed trickle of falling water and the vivid colours of the Koi. Outlook is an evocative space for contemplation, a landscape that both surprises and centers one through nature.

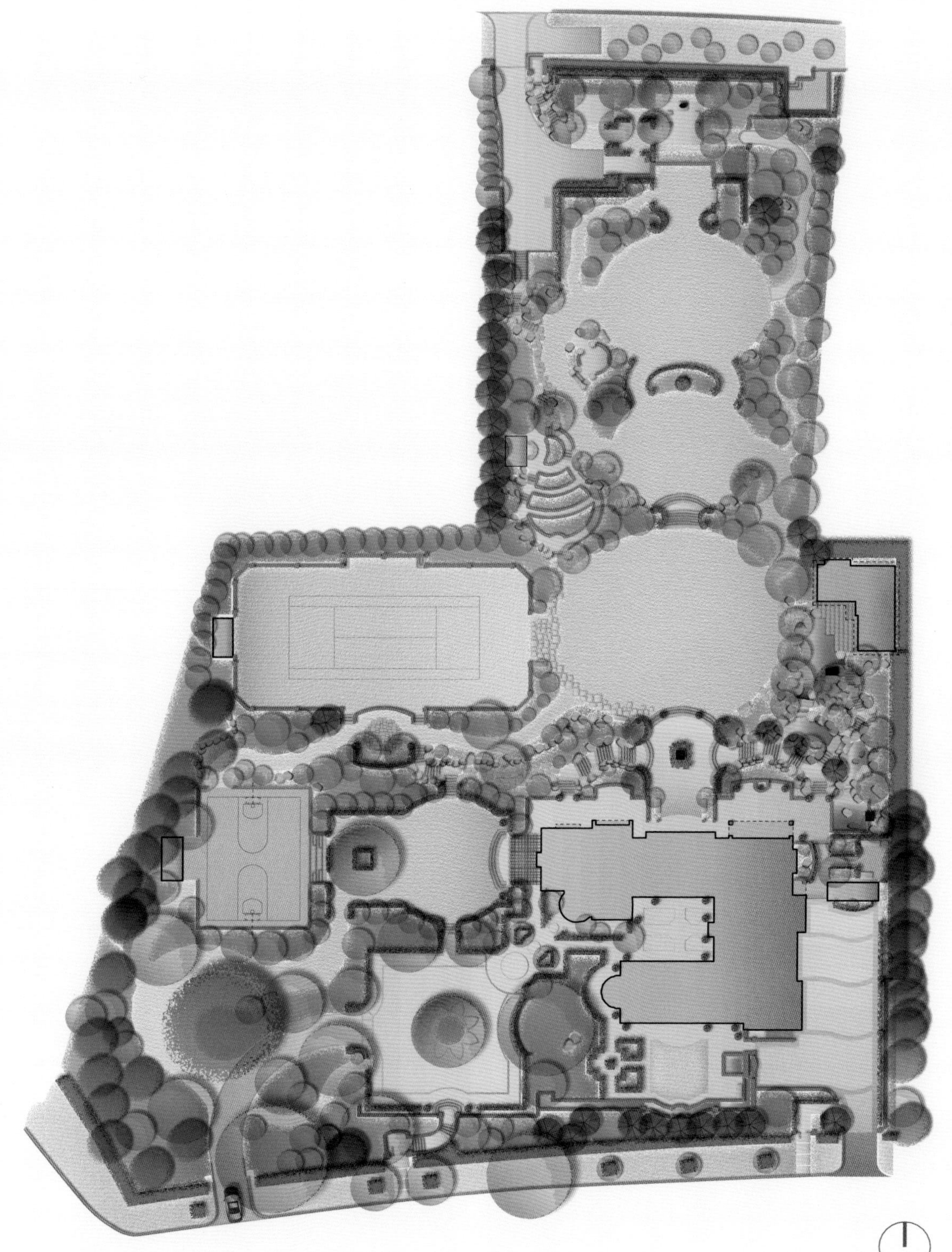

Far Above. Entry stairs spill into the entry court.

Above. A large Red Sunset Maple (*Acer rubrum 'Red sunset'*) provides a focal point in the entry court.

Left. The main entry reflects the conceptual importance of the garden to the site's layout, with its oblique axial approach and human scale canopy focusing attention on the landscape.

Left, Above and Right. Clipped Boxwood (*Buxus*) hedges define hard surfaces from the garden beds while specimen White Oak (*Quercus alba*), Maple (*Acer*), Southern Magnolia (*Magnolia grandiflora*) and Golden Robinia (*Robinia pseudoacacia 'Frisia'*) accentuate the entry court.

Left. A clipped Boxwood (*Buxus*) hedge echoes the classical form of the conservatory in the landscape.

Above. Golden Honey Locust (*Robinia pseudoacacia 'Frisia'*) anchors the terminus of an axial path.

Above. A mature White Oak (*Quercus alba*) arches gracefully over the residence, providing scale.

Next Spread. Paperbark Maple (*Acer griseum*) frame a large garden urn.

Left. Stone slab stairs spill down to the formal lawn anchored by a specimen Kobus Magnolia (*Magnolia kobus*) and down to the sport court.

Above. Colourful blossoms of Black Eyed Susan (*Rudebeckia*) enliven the colour garden lawn. Golden Honey Locust (*Robinia pseudoacacia* 'Frisia') rises from behind pleached trees, drawing the eye across the space.

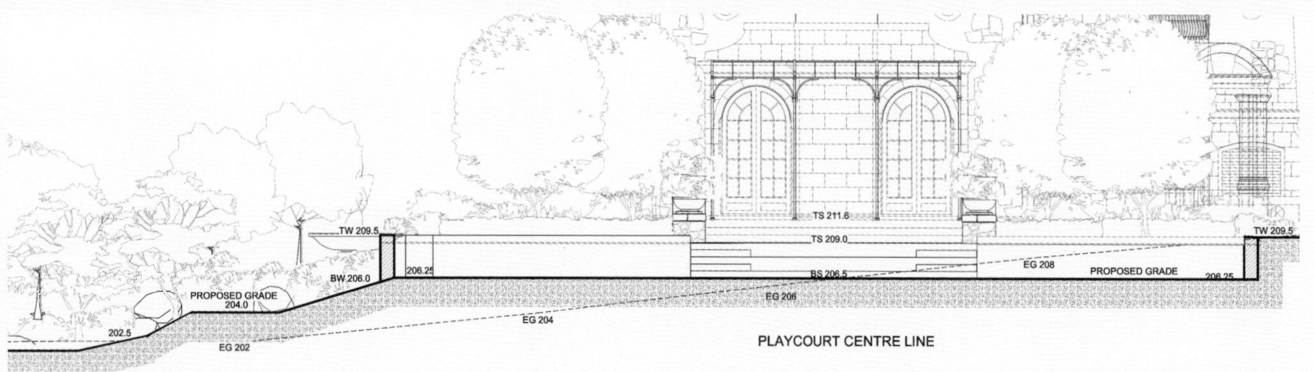
TW 209.5
TS 211.6
TS 209.0
TW 209.5
206.25
BW 206.0
EG 208
BS 206.5
PROPOSED GRADE
206.25
PROPOSED GRADE
204.0
EG 206
EG 204
202.5
EG 202
PLAYCOURT CENTRE LINE

Left. Contemporary stairs provide seating for the sport court off the formal lawn terrace.

Right. Black Eyed Susan (*Rudebeckia*) frame the view into the entry court.

Next Spread. Luxurious foliage, textures and colours cascade down a hillside to the viewing terrace and lawn tennis court.

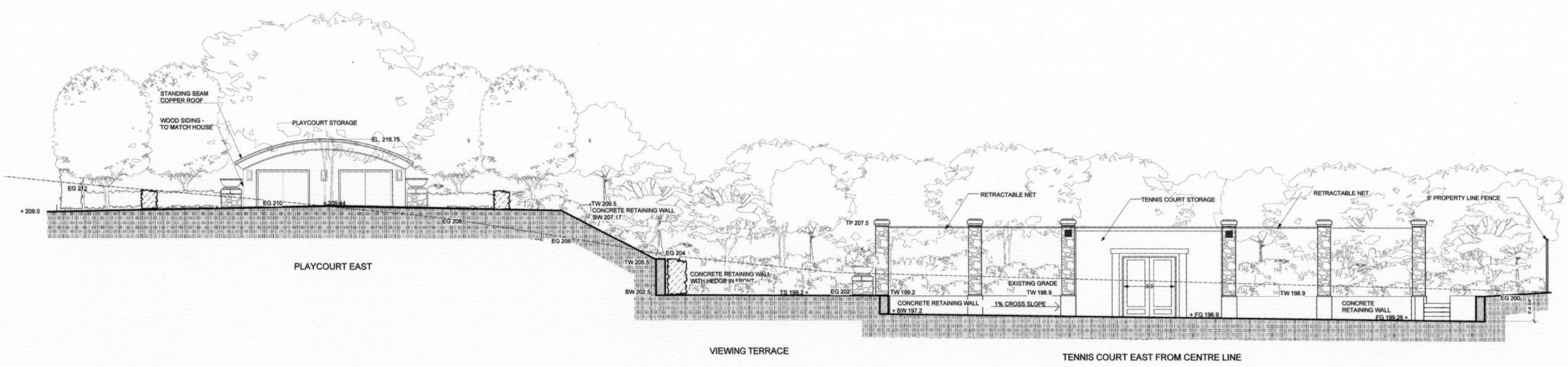

ELEVATION 'KK'
TENNIS COURT - WEST

Above. The lawn tennis court archway frames the leaves of Japanese Maple (*Acer palmatum* 'Suminagashi'), with Golden Honey Locust (*Robinia pesudoacacia* 'Frisia') accentuating depth of field. Stone clad walls transition to crisp concrete, linking the rough and the refined.

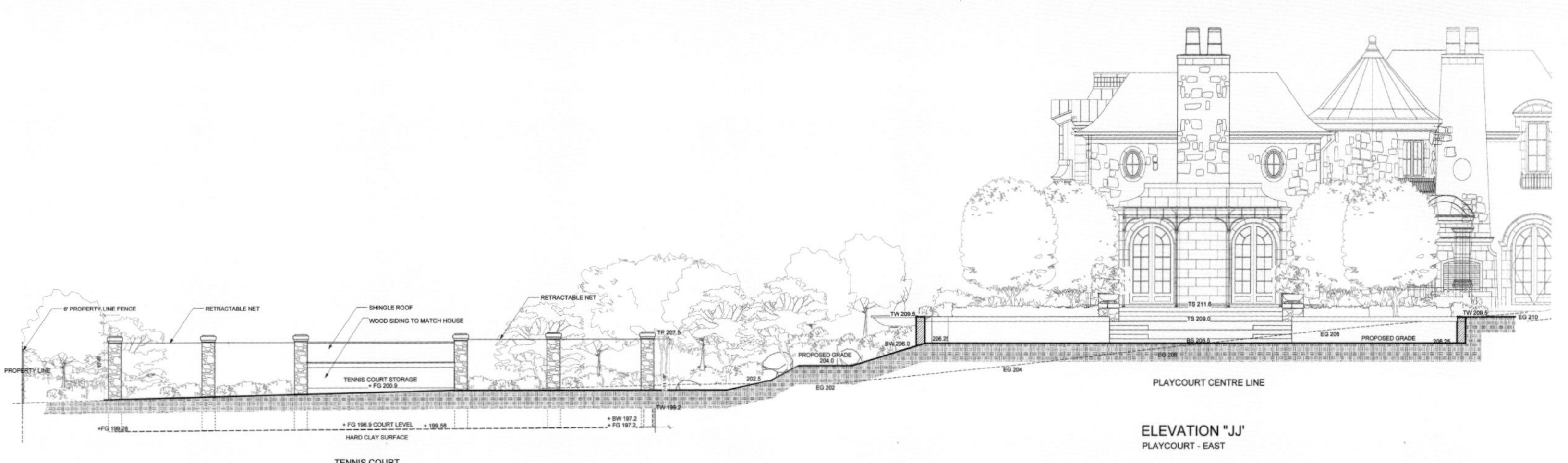
6' PROPERTY LINE FENCE
RETRACTABLE NET
SHINGLE ROOF
WOOD SIDING TO MATCH HOUSE
RETRACTABLE NET
PROPERTY LINE
TP 207.5
TENNIS COURT STORAGE
+ FG 200.9
TW 199.2
+ BW 197.2
+ FG 197.2
+ FG 196.9 COURT LEVEL
+ 199.58
+FG 199.28
HARD CLAY SURFACE
TENNIS COURT
TW 209.5
BW 206.0
206.25
PROPOSED GRADE
204.0
202.5
EG 202
EG 204
TS 211.6
TS 209.0
BS 206.5
EG 206
EG 208
PROPOSED GRADE
206.25
TW 209.5
EG 210
PLAYCOURT CENTRE LINE
ELEVATION "JJ'
PLAYCOURT - EAST

Left. Complimentary texture, sculptural form and varied colours reflect the attention given to tree selection throughout the property. The Japanese Maple (*Acer palmatum*) allows the residence to fade into the background, protecting the intimacy of the space.

Right. Sandstone stairs cascade through carefully selected plantings. Their form, texture and mature size enhancing the views while preserving sightlines.

Above. Golden light filters through a Red Japanese Maple (*Acer palmatum 'Atropurpureum'*) on to a stone slab path.

Left. Carefully placed boulders frame a Koi pond surrounded by Red Japanese Maples (*Acer palmatum 'Atropurpureum', Acer japonicum 'Aconitifolium', Acer palmatum 'Sangukaku', Acer palmatum 'Shishigashura', Acer palmatum 'Dissectum'*). The adjacent deck floats lightly over the surface of the water, providing a shady refuge for the Koi.

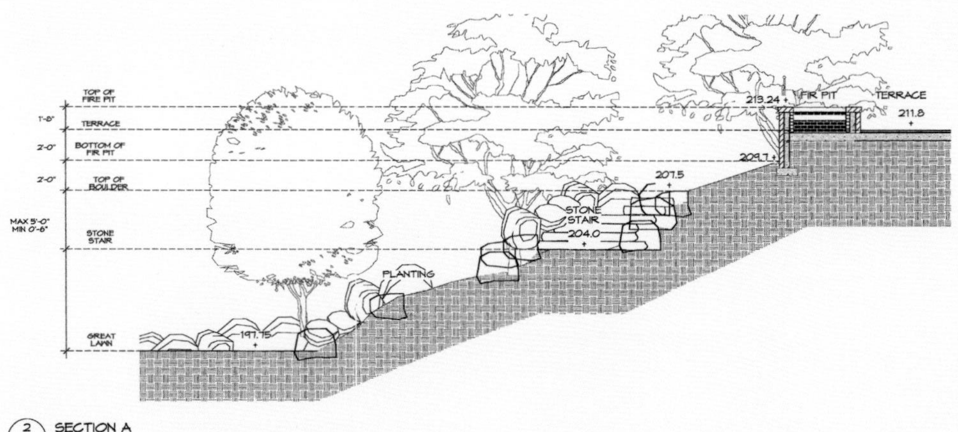

Above and Right. Waterfalls cascade over natural basalt boulders hand selected at the local quarry.

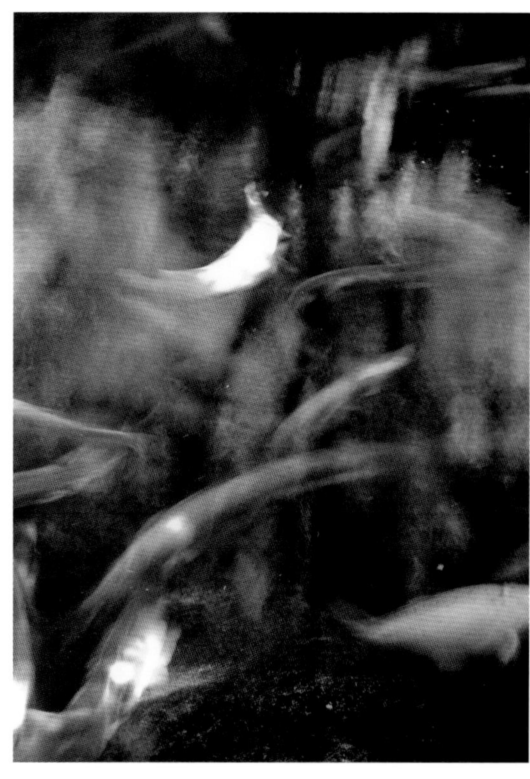

Above. Koi fish.

Left. A sensitively placed sculpture of a seated figure rests peacefully in the shade of a Japanese Maple tree *(Acer palmatum)*.

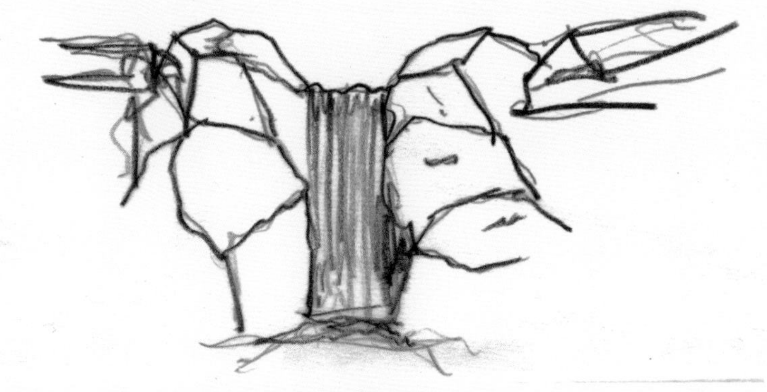

Above Right. A crisp clipped hedge provides a clean backdrop for the natural basalt boulders that frame a waterfall.

Right. Water feature concept sketch.

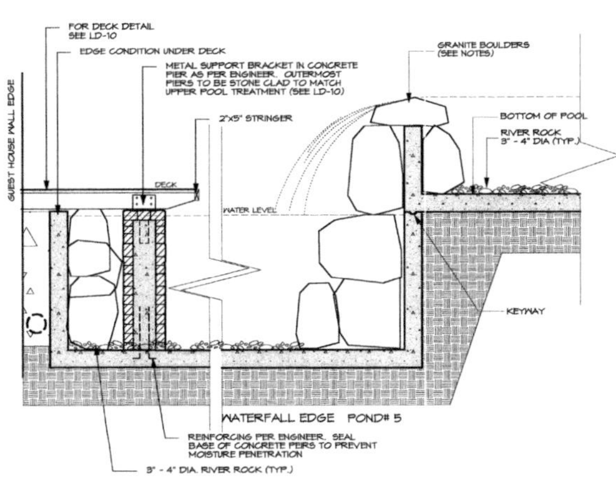

3 LD12 TYPICAL SECTION THROUGH POND # 5
SCALE : 3/8"=1'-0"

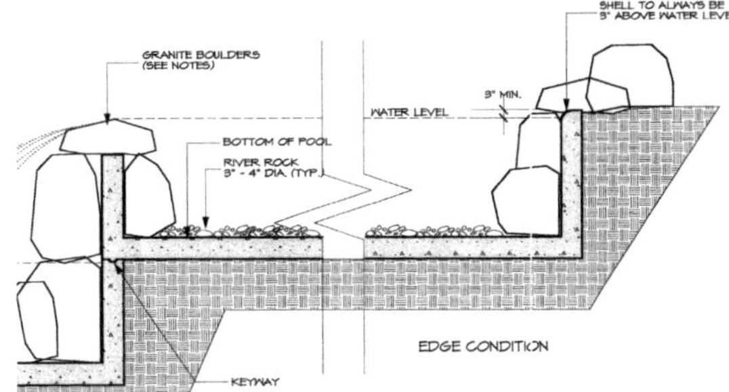

4 LD 12 TYPICAL SECTION THROUGH PONDS
SCALE : 3/8" = 1'-0"

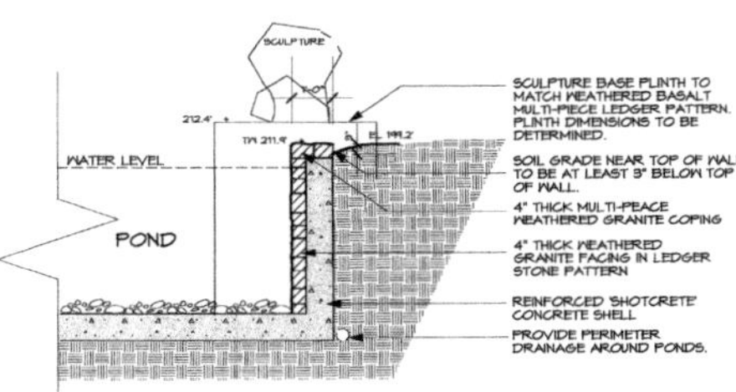

EDGE CONDITION AT SCULTURE
BASE IN UPPER POND

5 LD12 TYPICAL SECTION THROUGH POND # 1
SCALE : 3/8"=1'-0"

Left and Above. Carefully selected and placed basalt boulders guide the water course to the Koi pond.

Above and Right. A variety of garden walkways provide unique experiences of scent, colour and texture.

Left and Above. Numerous places to pause and sit continually reward and surprise.

12 LD8.2 ELEVATION METAL RAILING ENTRY STAIR
SCALE : 1/2"=1'-0"

11 LD8.2 ELEVATION METAL RAILING WEST TERRACE
SCALE : 1/2"=1'-0"

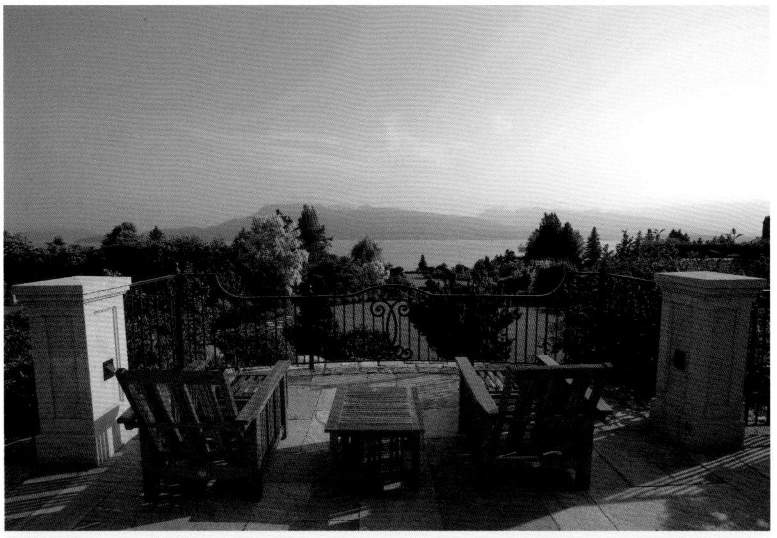

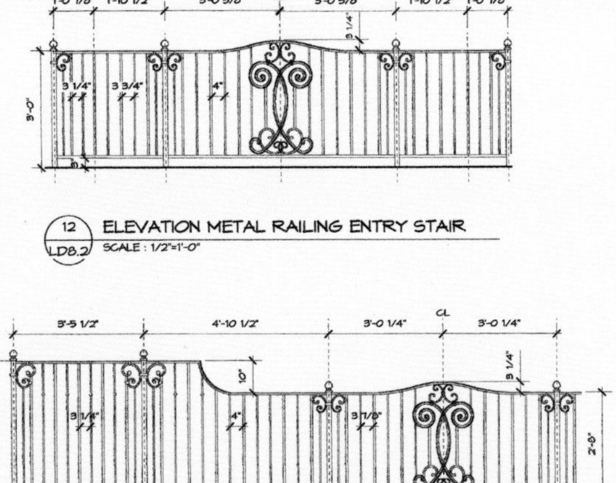

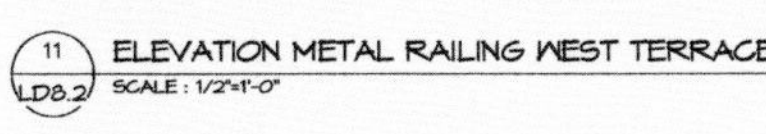

Above. The viewing terrace provides an intimate vantage point to the garden and Northshore Mountains.

Right. Planting and the framed openings to the lawn terraces create a forced perspective to the vista beyond.

Next Spread. Clipped Boxwood (*Buxus*) hedges, exuberant Peegee Hydrangeas (*Hydrangea paniculata*) and a lush canopy embrace the terraced oval lawns as they roll away from the French country influenced residence.

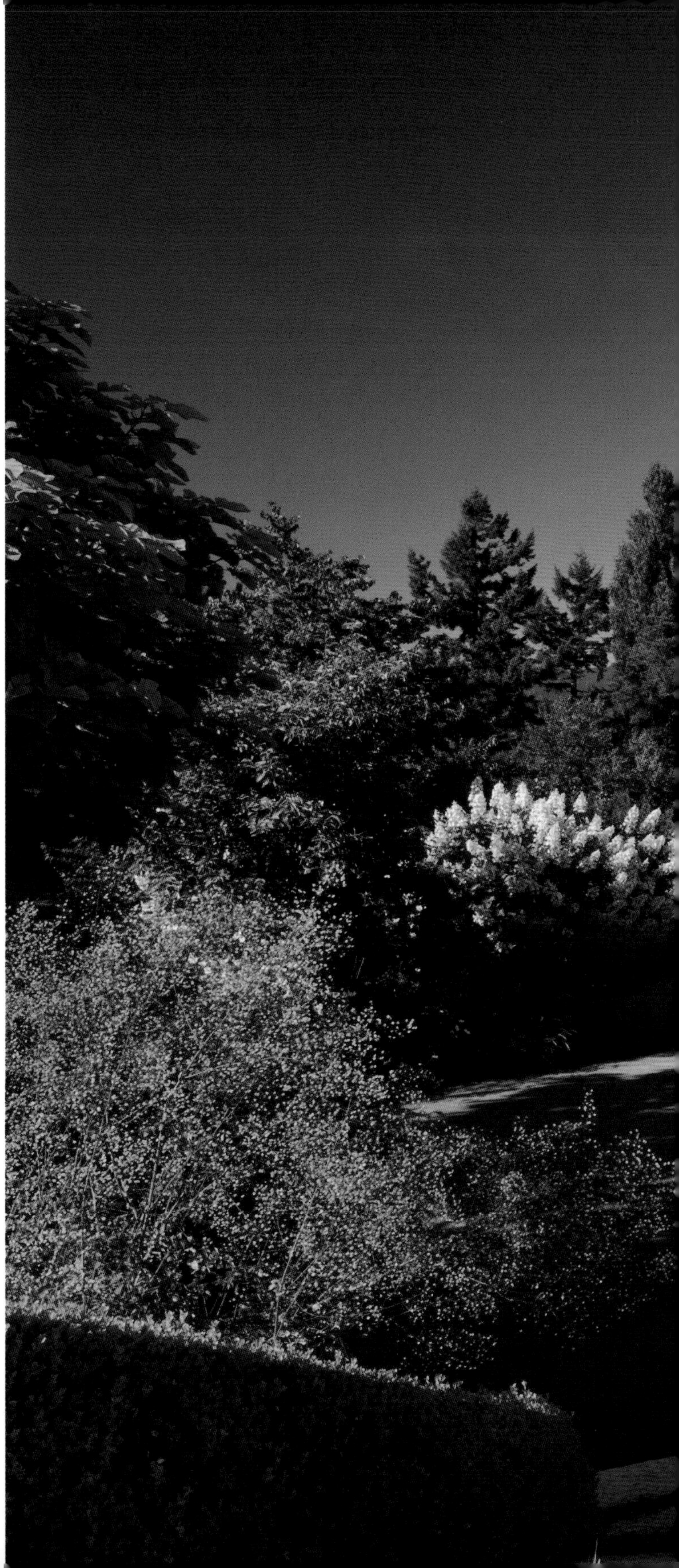

Above. An intimate path connects the upper and lower terraces of the compound.

Right. Formal sandstone stairs cascade between the south and central terraces of the great lawn, with roughly textured risers and natural boulders providing a foil for their classical form. Trees selected for their range of colour draw the eye into the surrounding spaces.

Left. The bottlebrush flower spikes of Black Bugbane (*Actea racemosa*), float in the ocean breeze.

Right. Late summer blooms of Anemone *(Anemone)* and Peegee Hydrangea *(Hydrangea paniculata)* frame a view of the grand staircase.

Above. The low canopy provides a frame for the great lawn while preserving sightlines to the view beyond. The trees shelter intimate pathways that wind through the planted border.

Right. An intimate path and staircase connects upper and lower terraces on the north side of the residence. Borrowed views from the surrounding landscape expand the sense of space.

BEFORE & AFTER

EAGLE WEST

11. URBAN RETREAT

The garden at Urban Retreat is a smartly tailored landscape on a compact lot. Entering through the front gate, a small, intimate courtyard sits directly in front of the house. The courtyard is made of 4' by 4' paving units with vivid green moss growing in the joints. A stand of Paperbark Maple trees (*Acer griseum*) creates an airy, light canopy and a soft feeling of enclosure. Though the space is markedly private, it remains in dialogue with the street. Two peek-a-boo views, cast between hedges, offer passers-by momentary glimpses into the garden and bring colourful vignettes of the street scene into the hushed enclave.

Stretching from the front gate entrance, a textured concrete walkway follows a tall hedgerow as it continues past the main side entry to a blue-tiled plunge pool, an herb garden, and a backyard terrace. A steel blue mesh railing lines the terrace, which features an outdoor eating area that connects to the kitchen inside. Nearly flush with the railing, bamboo waves in the wind, seeming to extend the space of the terrace. A cantilevered stairway leads down to a lower courtyard, where Black Bamboo (*Phyllostachys nigra*) grows. The plant is contained in pots in the ground with local basalt covering the surface of the soil. Glass doors open from the client's office out to the courtyard, offering a contemplative respite from work.

The entire space of the garden feels like a respite, a refuge from the city. Its mostly green and blue palette is cool and calming, and its organic play of the line—like the planted paver joints and the bamboo stalks reaching to the sky—is refreshing. The space feels not just relaxing, but restorative.

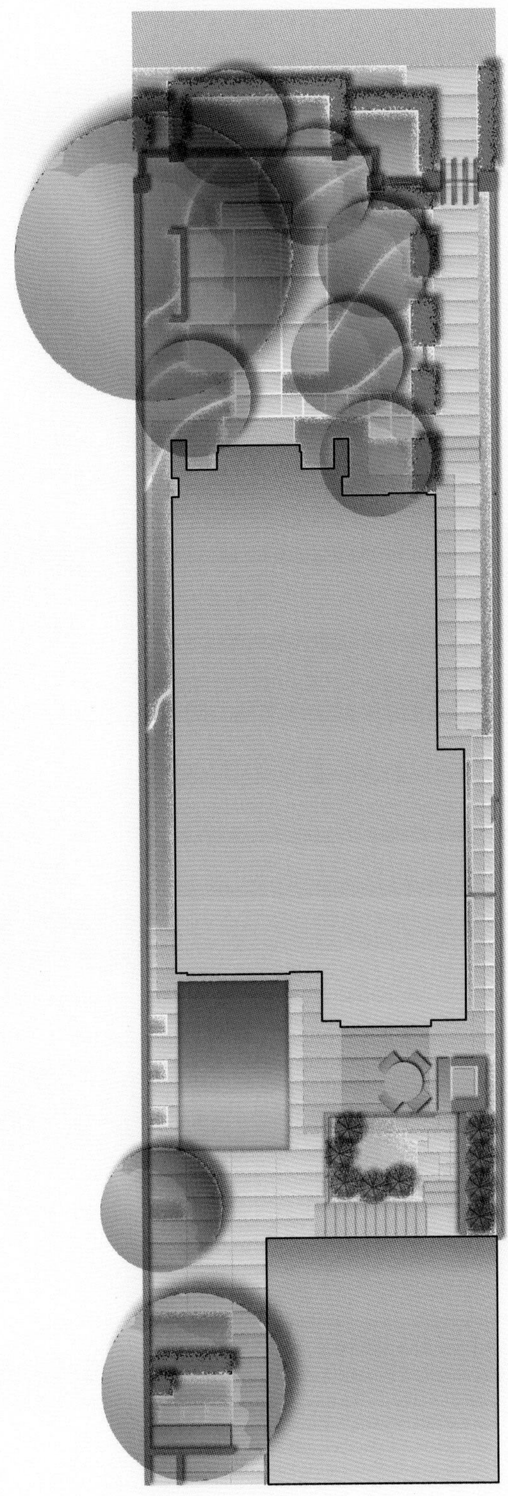

1918

Left and Above. Layered architecture and plantings harmonize with brick masonry walls.

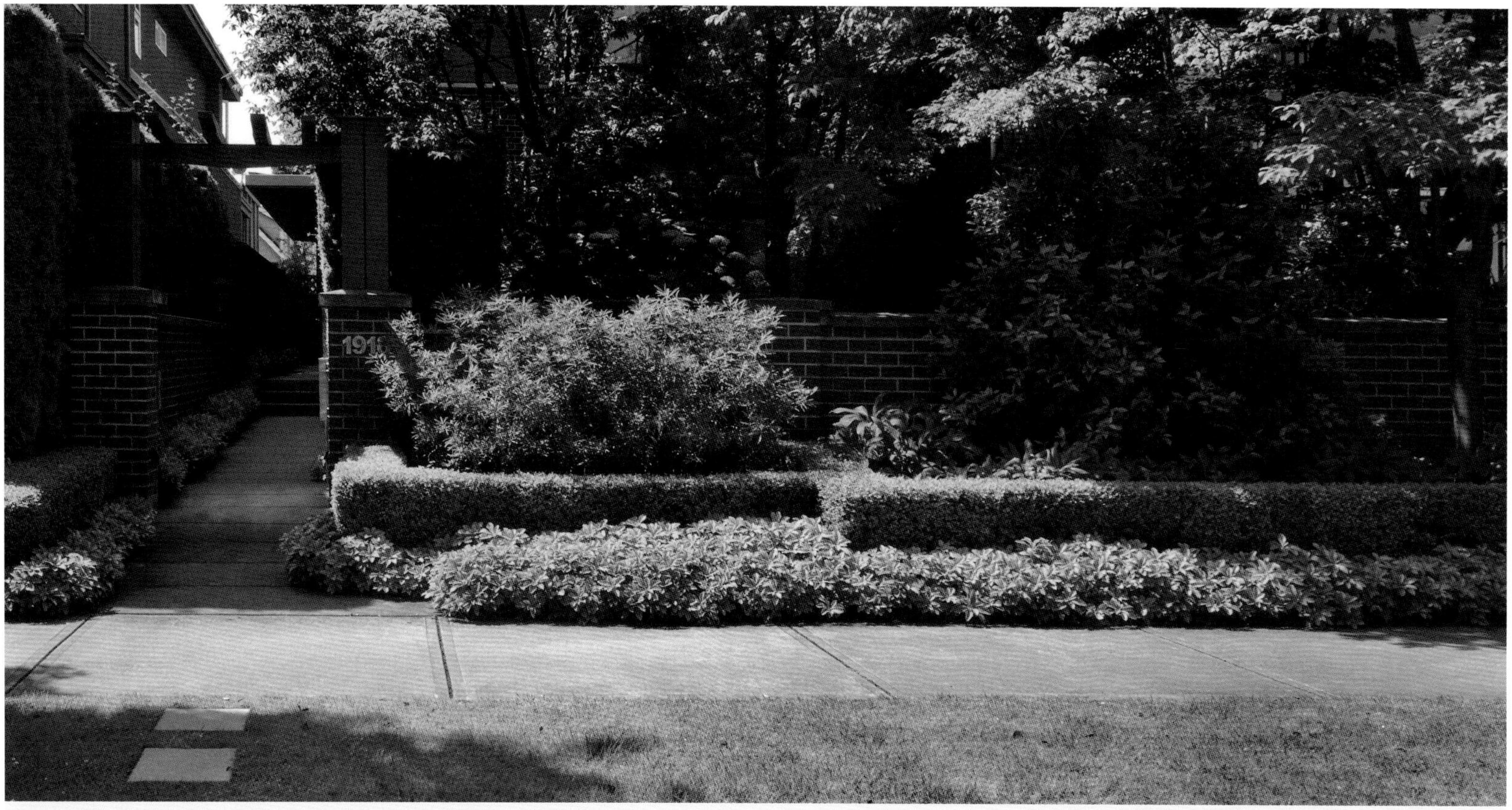

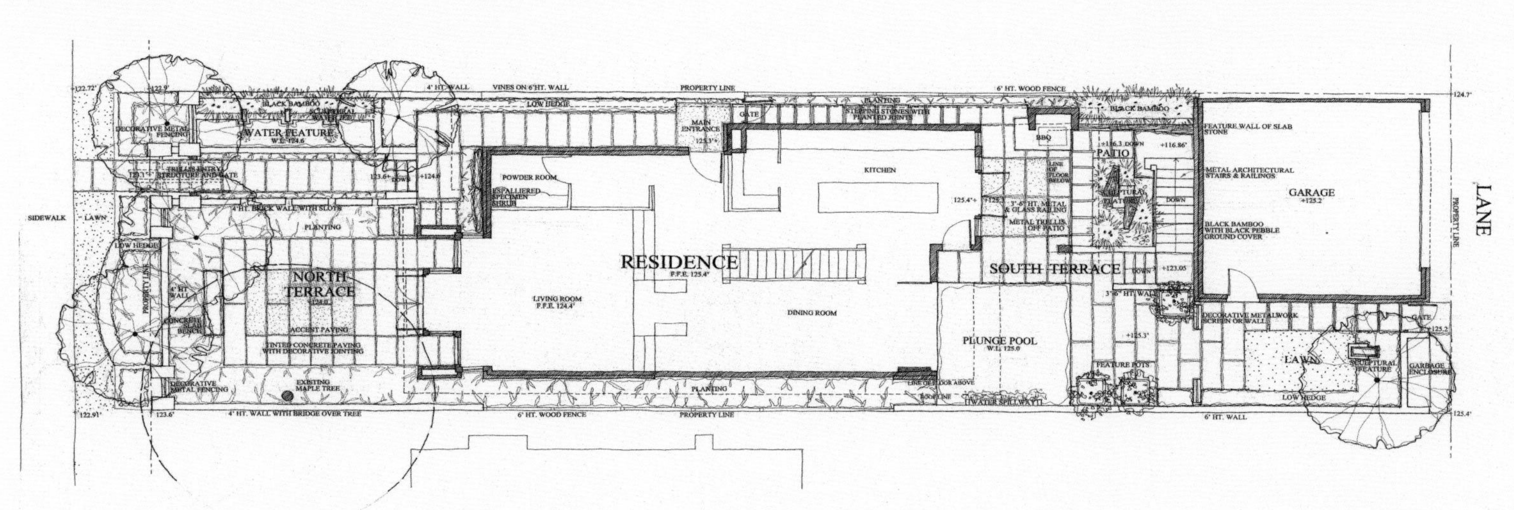

RESIDENCE
NORTH TERRACE
SOUTH TERRACE
PLUNGE POOL
GARAGE
LANE
PATIO
KITCHEN
LIVING ROOM
DINING ROOM
POWDER ROOM
MAIN ENTRANCE
WATER FEATURE
SIDEWALK
LAWN
LOW HEDGE
PLANTING
PROPERTY LINE
BLACK BAMBOO
6' HT. WOOD FENCE
6' HT. WALL
VINES ON 6' HT. WALL
4' HT. WALL WITH BRIDGE OVER TREE
ACCENT PAVING
TINTED CONCRETE PAVING WITH DECORATIVE JOINTING
EXISTING MAPLE TREE
DECORATIVE METAL FENCING
FEATURE WALL OF SLAB STONE
METAL ARCHITECTURAL STAIRS & RAILINGS
BLACK BAMBOO WITH BLACK PEBBLE GROUND COVER
DECORATIVE METALWORK SCREEN OR WALL
SCULPTURAL FEATURE
GARBAGE ENCLOSURE
FEATURE POTS
GATE
BBQ

Above. Metal picket openings feature vignettes into the interior courtyard along the entry walk.

Left. Conceptual garden plan.

Right. Yew (*Taxus*) create rhythmic architectural forms leading to the entry.

Left. Phormium in zinc planters create a rhythmic back-drop along the pool deck.

Above Right. Open stair risers allow for views through, expanding the sense of light and space.

Right. Pool and planter details.

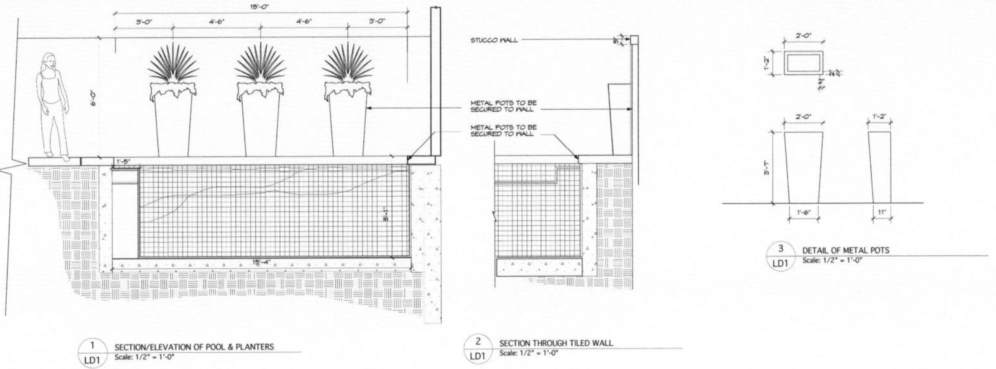

1 LD1 SECTION/ELEVATION OF POOL & PLANTERS
Scale: 1/2" = 1'-0"

2 LD1 SECTION THROUGH TILED WALL
Scale: 1/2" = 1'-0"

3 LD1 DETAIL OF METAL POTS
Scale: 1/2" = 1'-0"

Above. Folding doors open interior spaces to the outdoors and an inviting dip into the tiled plunge pool.

Right. Evergreen Magnolia (*Magnolia grandiflora*) and Bay Laurel (*Laurus nobilis*) provide a textural, evergreen canopy framing the edges of the pool deck.

Above and Right. Cantilevered stairs float through a sunken courtyard behind a filigree of Black Bamboo (*Phyllostachys nigra*).

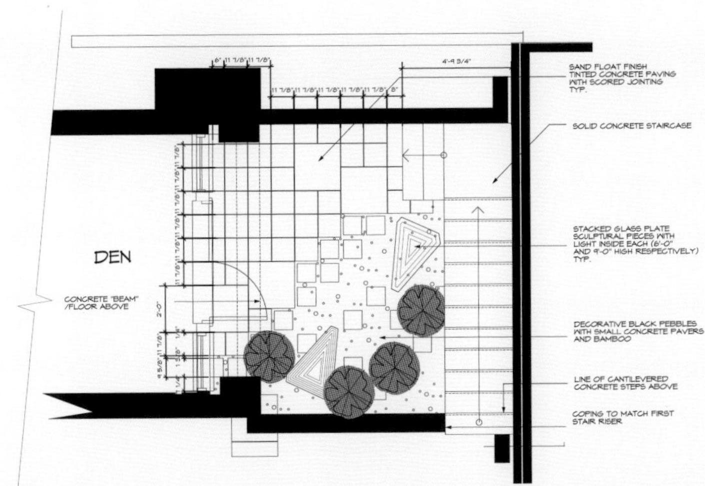

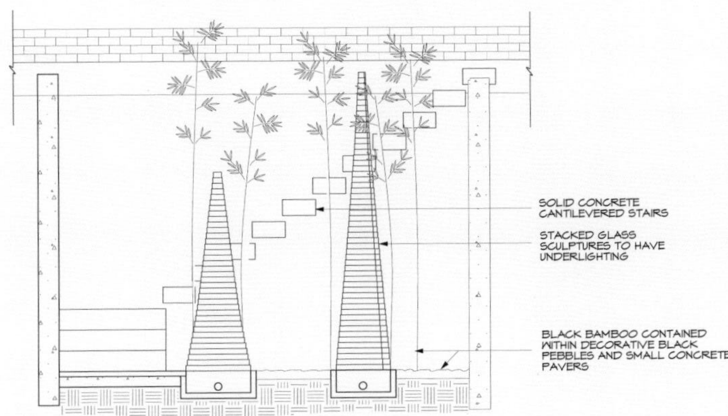

4 / LD1 SECTION/ELEVATION OF SUNKEN COURTYARD
Scale: 1/2" = 1'-0"

Above. Plan and elevation for sunken study courtyard.

Right. Black Bamboo (*Phyllostachys nigra*) and concrete, masonry and metal screens provide for subtle textural interplay.

Above and Right. Architecture and garden are woven together by layered plantings of Paperbark Maple (*Acer griseum*) and a textural understorey.

Left. Paperbark Maples (*Acer griseum*) are backdropped by the crisp line of Yew (*Taxus*) hedge and Hydrangeas.

Right. Paperbark Maples (*Acer griseum*) cast dappled light into the living room terrace.

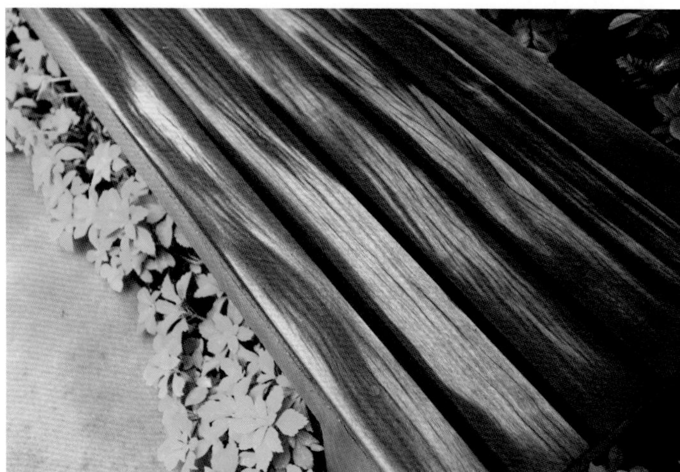

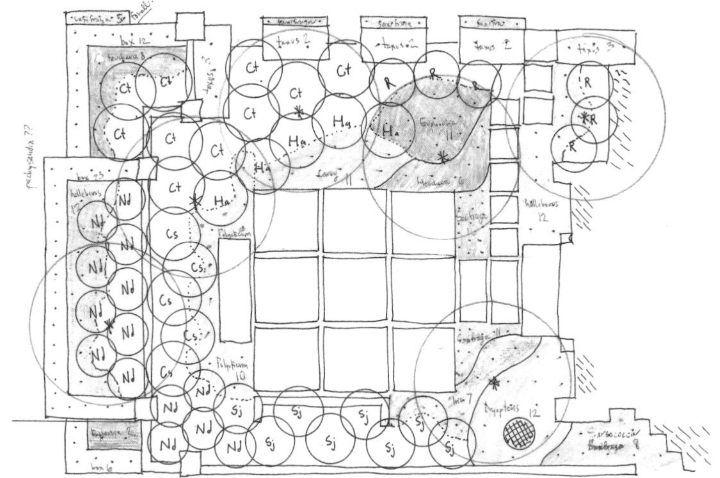

Above. Planting plan living room terrace.

Left. Wide planted joints and geometric concrete paving weave garden and hardscape together in this intimate terrace.

Right. Ipe and concrete bench detail.

Next Spread. A simple Ipe and concrete bench invites quiet contemplation in the rich and textural plantings of the living room terrace.

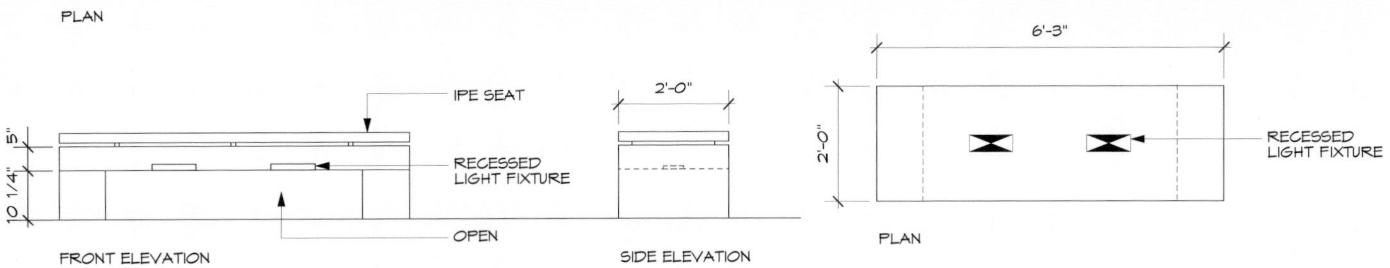
PLAN
IPE SEAT
5"
10 1/4"
RECESSED
LIGHT FIXTURE
OPEN
FRONT ELEVATION
2'-0"
SIDE ELEVATION
6'-3"
2'-0"
RECESSED
LIGHT FIXTURE
PLAN

BEFORE & AFTER

CRAFTING

12. EDGEWATER

On an Oceanside property, the garden of Edgewater is a built landscape in conversation with the natural and urban scenery of Vancouver's English Bay. A lawn terrace creates a visual trajectory between the lawn and the green mossy rocks of the coastline, and at high tide, the infinity pool terrace above the lawn visually connects to the ocean. A glass wall, a design element carried from the predominantly glass house to the landscape design, lines the edge of the property, allowing an unobstructed view of the peaks as well as passing sailboats. Limestone pavers extend from the inside of the home through the garden all the way to the glass wall, creating a strong linear pull that both draws the eye out and makes the garden look longer.

The staggered line of the garden's edge wall, a horizontal sculpture of a woman resting on her side, and boldly coloured low-lying plants, like a red-leafed Japanese Maple (*Acer palmatum dissectum*), draw interest to the immediate space, creating a visual specificity to the garden that is captivating. The juxtaposition of the sharp, rectilinear forms of the planting beds and water features and the loose, fluid shapes of the coastline and mountain ridge is a dichotomy that heightens through contrast the visceral pleasure of each.

The play between opacity and translucence—the strategic use of clear and sometimes frosted glass, the limpid water of the pool, stone walls, and tall, dense hedges—in both the garden and architecture creates a world that carefully curates what is seen and what is not seen, also evoking the clear, luminous ocean and the solid barrier of the mountains.

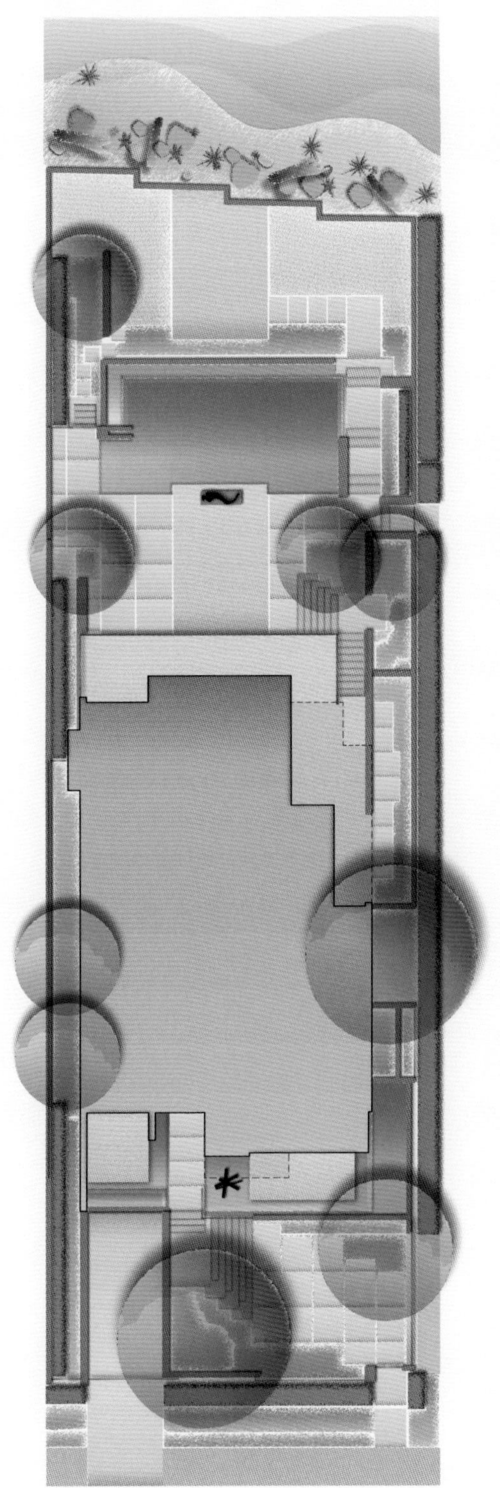

Above. The organic forms of plants provide a foil for the strong geometry of the architecture.

Left. Viewed from the street, the residence rises above the Yew hedge. The pedestrian gate and architectural details refine the composition, adding interest and definition to the simplicity of the rectilinear volumes.

Above. Cantilevered limestone stairs appear to float over a bed of Spurge (*Euphorbia*).

Next Spread. Paperbark Maple (*Acer griseum*) and an abstract John Henry sculpture contrast with the fine, grey finish of architectural concrete.

Above. Recalling the form and colour of the Native Arbutus (*Arbutus menziesii*) a specimen Paperbark Maple (*Acer griseum*) acts as an anchor and formal foil in the entry courtyard.

Left. Morning light and the sculptural form of plants animate the water feature.

Above. Clear contrast of texture, form and colour express a focused design intent.

Right. Crisp forms and smooth textures define the entry.

Left and Above. After a summer rain, the clean lines of the hardscape are punctuated by the reflected sculpture.

Next Spread. The articulated volumes of the entry court and east elevation of the residence allow for a play of light and shadow. Semi-private and private space are subtly defined through the integration of low walls and partitions.

Right. A Weeping Red Japanese Maple (*Acer palmatum dissectum 'Ever red'*) provides an organic sculptured counterpoint to the refined concrete stairs from the living terrace to the pool terrace.

Left. With a verdant planting framing its boundary, the Jewel-like quality of the pool's glass tile is heightened.

Above Right. A sculptural approach is expressed at every level of detail.

Right. Planting plan.

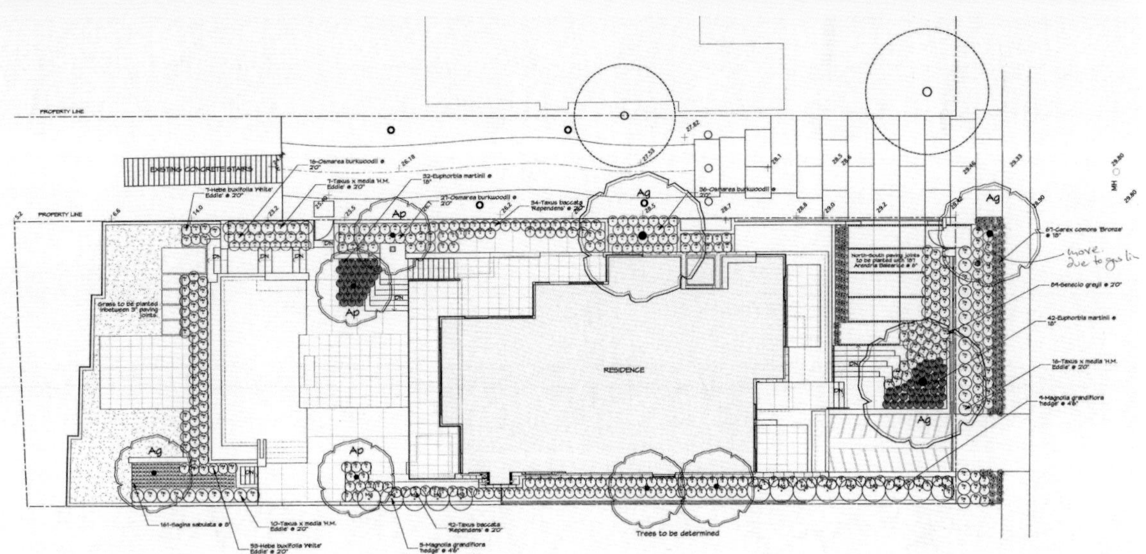
PROPERTY LINE
EXISTING CONCRETE STAIRS
16-Osmarea burkwoodii @ 2'0"
7-Taxus x media 'H.M. Eddie' @ 2'0"
32-Euphorbia martinii @ 18"
7-Hebe buxifolia 'White' Eddie' @ 2'0"
27-Osmarea burkwoodii @ 2'0"
34-Taxus baccata 'Rependens' @ 2'0"
36-Osmarea burkwoodii @ 2'0"
PROPERTY LINE
Ap
Ag
Grass to be planted inbetween 3" paving joints.
RESIDENCE
North-South paving joints to be planted with 187 Arendria Balearica @ 6"
67-Carex comons 'Bronze' @ 18"
move due to gas lin
84-Senecio greyii @ 2'0"
42-Euphorbia martinii @ 18"
16-Taxus x media 'H.M. Eddie' @ 2'0"
9-Magnolia grandiflora 'hedge' @ 4'6"
161-Sagina subulata @ 8"
10-Taxus x media 'H.M. Eddie' @ 2'0"
53-Hebe buxifolia 'White' Eddie' @ 2'0"
42-Taxus baccata 'Rependens' @ 2'0"
5-Magnolia grandiflora 'hedge' @ 4'6"
Trees to be determined
MH

Left. Emphasizing the axial relationship of residence to the mountain view, stone paving cuts a crisp line through the manicured lawn and pool terrace.

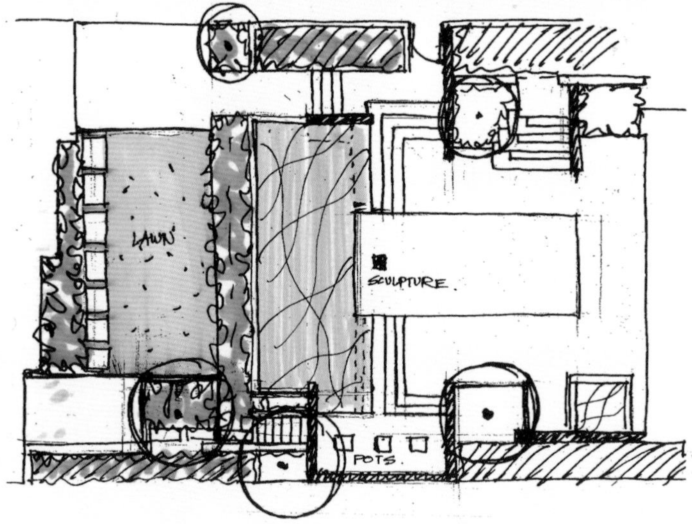

Above. Schematic concept plan.

Far Above and Right. The garden's refined abstraction of the spectacular view is clearly represented in the terrace's textures, forms, patterns and colours.

Left and Above. Organic and rectilinear forms harmonize within the shared frame of the garden and view.

Next Spread. A bronze sculpture from the client's collection provides scale to an everchanging view.

BEFORE & AFTER

THE EPIPHANY

BY PAUL SANGHA

My work reflects a deep-seated love of the inner calm that can be provided by a journey through a garden. My obsession with detail is part of that journey. It is through meticulous detailing that I feel the eye and mind can avoid being jarred by the flaws and thoughtlessness of someone who does not care to consider each moment of experience. I lay out gardens to embrace fluidity as a form of movement, reflecting that life is a journey that you do not backtrack on, but ultimately cycles back around so that one can experience it again and hopefully appreciate the next time what was not there for them during their first experience. Scents, light, seasons, colours, sounds, and time are ever changing in the garden to different degrees. I do not know how many times I have already taken this journey but I do know this particular one continues to grow richer with every experience, and I would like to express my sincerest gratitude for this time on the path together.

APPENDIX

BIOGRAPHY

Paul Sangha has been creating timeless landscapes for over 25 years, and is widely regarded as Vancouver's premier residential Landscape Architect.

Paul Sangha is an alumnus of UBC and graduated as the distinguished Dr. John Wesley Neill Medalist. Paul has returned to UBC both as an adjunct professor and on the advisory panel for the School of Architecture and Landscape Architecture. In support of the school he has established a scholarship for Design Excellence in Landscape Architecture and has committed to an annual lecture to bring international speakers to Vancouver.

Paul Sangha Landscape Architecture was established in 1999 after a 3.5-year partnership, prior to which he worked as a senior Landscape Architect and designer for 10 years.

Paul Sangha is passionate about design, about the possibilities for uniting architecture, nature, and design in creating highly individual gardens and experiences.

Paul Sangha's landscape designs result from a rigorous and collaborative design process, one that is grounded in an understanding of each site and the desires of the client. Intrinsic to his design process is a belief in sustainability and community; as such, he continually strives to express his designs and ideas through minimal brush strokes.

Paul Sangha's aim is simple: to design beautiful natural environments that inspire and refresh those who use them.

ACKNOWLEDGEMENT

I would like to express my sincerest gratitude for the gracious patronage of my wonderful clients and the opportunity to work with amazing architects, interior designers, contractors and craftsmen. Only through the support of my wife, Goldie, and daughters, Tasha and Riva, was I able to pursue my obsession and passion for design.

AWARDS

1990-2013

2013 – Canadian Society of Landscape Architects
• Regional Honour, Creek's End

2012 – Canadian Society of Landscape Architects.
• Regional Merit, Tolmie House

2012 – Masonry Design Awards
• Tolmie House

2011 – Western Living Designers of the Year Awards
• Landscape Designer of the Year

2010 – BC Landscape Award of Excellence
• Spanish Banks Private Estate

2008 – Landscape Award for Excellence
• 6476 Blenheim Street

2008 – Georgie Award
• 6287 MacDonald St. Van, Bryan Residence

2007 January – Established the Paul Sangha Limited Scholarship in Design Excellence for the University of British Columbia's Landscape Architecture Program

2006 August 31 – BCLNA - BC Landscape and Nursery Association
• Judging Panel for "Landscape Awards of Excellence Competition"

2006 June – Vancouver Garden Club & Vancouver Park Board
• Judging Panel for "Upfront Garden's Competition"

2006 March 9 – Garden Club of Vancouver 'Pot Party'
• Donation of Pot & Planting arrangement for auction to benefit VanDusen Botanical Gardens 'Planting the Seed' Capital Campaign

2001 - Gardens of Vancouver
Judge for Gardening Competition

1998 – Georgie Award
• Residential Garden Design, Law Residence

1996 – Canadian Home Builders Association
• National Award of Excellence, Chow Residence

1995 – British Columbia Nursery Trade Association
• Award of Excellence, Leung Residence

1995 – British Columbia Nursery Trade Association
• Grand Prize for Scott Residence
• Award for 1239 Matthews Avenue Residence

1995 – Georgie Gold Award
• Residential Garden Design, 1864 Matthews Avenue

1995 – Northwest Flower and Garden Show, Seattle, Washington
• Gold Medal, Horticulture Magazine Award
• Gold Medal, The Arboretum Magazine Award
• Gold Medal, Centre for Urban Horticulture Award
• Silver Medal, Chelsea Award

1994 – Street of Dreams Awards
• Best of Show, Outstanding Achievement, The Sonoma

1994 – City of Vancouver Heritage Award
• 1864 Matthews Avenue

1994 – British Columbia Nursery Trade Association
• Residential Garden Design, McGavin Residence

1993 – Georgie Awards
• Ocean Point
• Pacifica

1993 – City of Vancouver Heritage Award
• Dukowski Residence

1991 – British Columbia Nursery Trade Association
• Grand Prize, Dragovan Residence

1991 – Canadian Society of Landscape Architects
• Regional Award, Tai Residence

1990 – Canadian Society of Landscape Architects
• Regional Award, 1365 West Broadway

PUBLICATIONS

1989-2013

Award Magazine
"The Kingswood" December 2000

Azure Design, Architecture and Art
"Who's Who in Vancouver Design" March/ April 1993

BC Home
"Dream House, Real House" November 2006

Builders Architect Magazine
Feature article & cover September 2004

Canadian Architect
"Building with Word" April 2006

Canadian Garden
"Common Grounds" June/July 1998
"Brick Beauties" April 1992

Canadian House and Home
"Best of all Worlds" October 2007
Canadian Gardener (CBC Television)
Spevakow Garden profiled July 1998

Canadian Gardening
"At-a-Glance" June 2008

Canadian House & Home
"Direction 1991" January 1991
"Estates of the Arts" June/July 1990

Canadian Living
"Grand Tours" February/March 1995
"The Garden Edge" March 1994

City & Country Home
"Dynamic New Directions Transform a Staid Vancouver Garden" April/May 1993

Creative Gardens & Landscapes 1998
Engagement Calendar

Design Quarterly
"Residential Gardens Growing in Popularity" Winter 2001

Dream House
"Pursuing the Dream House" March-April 2005

Dream Porches and Sunrooms (by Michael Snow)
p. 16, 64-69

Dwell In Nature: Poetic Gardens
Featured gardens, Hong Kong Architectural Press, 2012

Garden Design
"Home on the Hill: English Traditions Unite a British Columbia Residence" February/ March 1994

Gardens West
"Deck Design Tips" May 1997

Gardening Life
"In Sync" November/December 2001
"Natural Wonders" March/April 2005

Gray Magazine
"Sense of Place" Issue no. 7/61 December 2012

Horticulture: The Magazine of American Gardening
"The Color of Winter" Horticulture Magazine Award for 1995 Northwest Flower and Garden Show

Homes & Living Magazine
"Bryant house" August/September 2013

House and Garden
"The Green Glades of Home" November 1999

Hort West
"Grand Overall Award of Excellence"
Cover Photo, November/December 1996
"Landscape Award Winner"
September/ October 1994

Mehfil Magazine
"Putting a Green Thumb To Work" March 1997

Nuvo Magazine
"Magnificent Obsession" Winter 2000

Pacific Horticulture
"A Fine Marriage" Fall 1998

Step Magazine
"Heavenly Gates" July/September 1991

Style At Home
"A New Beginning" May 2004

Sunset Magazine
"A Shady Forest Glen in Vancouver, BC" August 1996

True West
"The Path to a Garden Classic is Paved With Gravel" May 1996

The Weekend Sun Newspaper
"Estates of Grace" August 7, 1993

Vancouver Sun Newspaper
"They're the Tops" June 16. 2006
"Growing With the Pros" March 2003
"Three Rs Hold the Key to Garden Renovation" January 2002
"It's Up To Us If We Want BC Gardens To Be Glorious" January, 1999
"Garden Notes" July 1995
"Seattle Show Organizers Find Themselves Grappling With Too Much Success" January 1995
"Street of Dreams – Best of Show Winners" September 1994
"Mansion-Makers Build Careers" September 1994
"The Art of Garden Design" April 1994
"Away with Lawns" August 1992
"Lavish Cottage-Style Garden Wins Top Landscaping Honor" December 1991
"Taking The Plunge" August 1991
"Hunting for Garden Treasures" August 1991
"Top Landscape Architects Issue Their Own Manifesto" July 1991
"Hampton Place Wins With a British Accent" 1991
"Gardens – the Greening of Paul Sangha" 1991

Water Garden: Landscape Design Series
Featured gardens, Hong Kong Architectural Press, 2012

Western Living
"Designers of the Year/Landscape/In His Element" September 2011 p. 86-87
"An Inside Job" September 2009 (Photography by Ed White) p. 58-62
"Green and Greener" August 2006
"Don't Worry, You'll See The Pavilion" June/July 2005
"Gardens of Good Taste" May 1995
"Towards a New Garden Style" May 1994
"Making a Shade Garden" May 1991
"Private Passions" May 1991
"A Princess in the Garden" August 1989

STAFF

CURRENT STAFF

Arteaga Melgoza, Mario
Bishop, David
Davis, Lara
Howu, Joe Chun Lung
Sangha, Paul
Srivastava, Mohit
Tanwar, Vikas
Vogt, Megan
Wu, Micole
Avideh Sheikh
Mahsa Azari
Jazmin Cendeno-Orozco

FORMER STAFF

Andrushko, Melanie
Bennett, Chloe
Bonde, Bhavana
Brewer, Brenda
Carver, Sarah
Charrey, Kaline
Demers, Dave
Downie, Amelia
Fielding, Bernice
Gentry, Anita
Green, Anita
Guppy, Blair
Burnett, Kacie
Jones, Helen
Kennedy, Claire
Kovar, Martin
Laing, Allison
Laing, Elizabeth
Lewinberg, Tanya
Mackay, Sharon
Main, Alan
Markham Zantvoort, Kate
McBeth, Laurie
McIntosh, Stewart
McMaster, Michelle
Nguyen, Elizabeth
Nielsen, Linda
Pang, Fanny
Pesa, Susanna
Reda, Vincenzo
Revoczi, Tamás
Sleigh, Dana
Stern, Yaron
Stewart, Ian
Turner, Wayne
Xu, Lu
Zygalo, Sylvia
Matthew, Tammyanne

CONTRIBUTORS

CAROLYN DEUSCHLE is a Master's of Landscape Architecture candidate at Harvard University Graduate School of Design. Previously an editor at Princeton Architectural Press in New York, Carolyn is interested in making the discourse surrounding landscape architecture more accessible to a mass audience. Her writing has appeared in *Landscape Architecture* magazine and on DesignObserver.com.

BYRON HAWES is a Toronto-based writer, who has lived and worked across the world. He writes primarily on architecture, design, fashion, and the arts, and has contributed to publications including *Architectural Digest, Azure, Wallpaper,* and *BlackBook,* amongst others.

NIC LEHOUX is a Canadian architectural photographer who works with architects that push the boundaries of design of the built environment. Nic is regularly commissioned to document significant buildings around the world with his unique eye, lighting and sense of composition. His images are frequently published in the international architectural press. His professional work puts a particular emphasis on incorporating people within tightly composed architectural photographs. Nic is influenced by the concept of the "decisive moment" popularized by Henry Cartier-Bresson which he adapts to the rigors of architectural photography. His images therefore serve as a reflection on the interaction of people with the built environment.

OSCAR RIERA OJEDA is an editor and designer based in Philadelphia, Singapore , and Buenos Aires. Born in 1966, in Argentina, he moved to the United States in 1990. Since then he has published over one hundred books, assembling a remarkable body of work notable for its thoroughness of content, timeless character, and sophisticated and innovative craftsmanship. Oscar Riera Ojeda's books have been published by many prestigious publishing houses across the world, including ORO editions, Birkhäuser, Byggförlaget, The Monacelli Press, Gustavo Gili, Thames & Hudson, Rizzoli, Whitney Library of Design, and Taschen. Oscar Riera Ojeda is also the creator of numerous architectural book series, including Ten Houses, Contemporary World Architects, The New American House and The New American Apartment, Architecture in Detail, and Single Building.

PROJECT **CREDITS**

REFLECTIONS
Architect: Unknown
Landscape Contractor: Fossil Project Services Ltd.
PSLA – Paul Sangha, Vikas Tanwar, Bernice Fielding, Kate Markham- Zantvoort, Elizabeth Laing

RAVINE'S EDGE
Original Architect: Arthur Erickson
General Contractor: Interior Craft Inc.
Landscape Contractor: Artistic Stoneworks Ltd.
PSLA – Paul Sangha, Mario Artega, Bernice Fielding, Elizabeth Laing

CLUB HOUSE
Architect: Formwerks Architectural Inc., Principal in charge, Howard Airey, (The Airey Group);
Sr. Designer, Alex Glegg (HenryGlegg Residential Design)
General Contractor: Keystone Construction Ltd.
Landscape Contractor: Artistic Stoneworks Ltd.
PSLA – Paul Sangha, Mario Artega, Claire Kennedy

CREEK'S END
Architect: Gordon Hlynsky Architect Inc.
General Contractor: Bradner Homes Ltd.
Landscape Contractor: Fossil Project Services Ltd.
PSLA – Paul Sangha, Mohit Srivastava, Vikas Tanwar, Bernice Fielding, Elizabeth Laing

TSAWWASSEN BLUFF
Architect: Grant Sinclair Architects
Landscape Contractor: Fossil Project Services Ltd.
PSLA – Paul Sangha, Mohit Srivastava, Elizabeth Laing, Bernice Fielding

UNFOLDED
Original
Architect: Robert Lemon Architect Inc.
General Contractor: Calrudd Construction Co. Ltd.
Landscape Renovations
Landscape Contractor: Fossil Project Services Ltd.
PSLA – Paul Sangha, Mohit Srivastava, Bernice Fielding

HILLSIDE JEWEL

Architect: Margot Innes Design
Interior Designer: Dennis Garritty
General Contractor: GemLevy Project Ltd.
Landscape Contractor: Trillium Landscaping Inc.
PSLA – Paul Sangha, Vikas Tanwar, Bernice Fielding, Kate Markham-Zantvoort, Elizabeth Laing

QUINTESSENTIAL

Original Installation
Architect: Ernest Collins Architect Ltd.
General Contractor: Gordon Wilson Construction Co. Ltd
Landscape Contractor: Allgreen Landscaping Ltd.
Rule Sangha and Associates Ltd. – Principal in charge, Paul Sangha
Renovations 2006
Landscape Contractor: Fossil Project Services Ltd.
PSLA - Paul Sangha, Bernice Fielding

TEXTURES

Architect: Hotson Bakker Boniface Haden Architects, Principals in charge, Alan Boniface, Bruce Haden; Sr. Architect, Andrew Larigakas
General Contractor: Gordon Wilson Construction Co. Ltd.
Landscape Contractor: Artistic Stoneworks Ltd.
PSLA – Paul Sangha, Sharon Mackay, Bhavana Bonde, Claire Kennedy

OUTLOOK

Architect: Formwerks Architectural Inc., Principal in charge, Howard Airey, (The Airey Group);
Sr. Architect, Kent Halex (Halex Architecture Ltd.)
General Contractor: Keystone Projects Ltd.
Landscape Contractor: Fossil Project Services Ltd.
PSLA – Paul Sangha, Mohit Srivastava, Claire Kennedy

URBAN RETREAT

Architect: Stuart Howard Architects Inc.
General Contractor: Meridian Pacific Construction Inc.
Landscape Contractor: Artistic Stoneworks Ltd.
PSLA – Paul Sangha, Sarah Carver, Claire Kennedy

EDGEWATER

Architect: Christopher Bozyk Architects Ltd.
General Contractor: Kindred Construction Ltd.
Landscape Contractor: Fossil Project Services Ltd.
PSLA – Paul Sangha, Bavana Bonde, Claire Kennedy

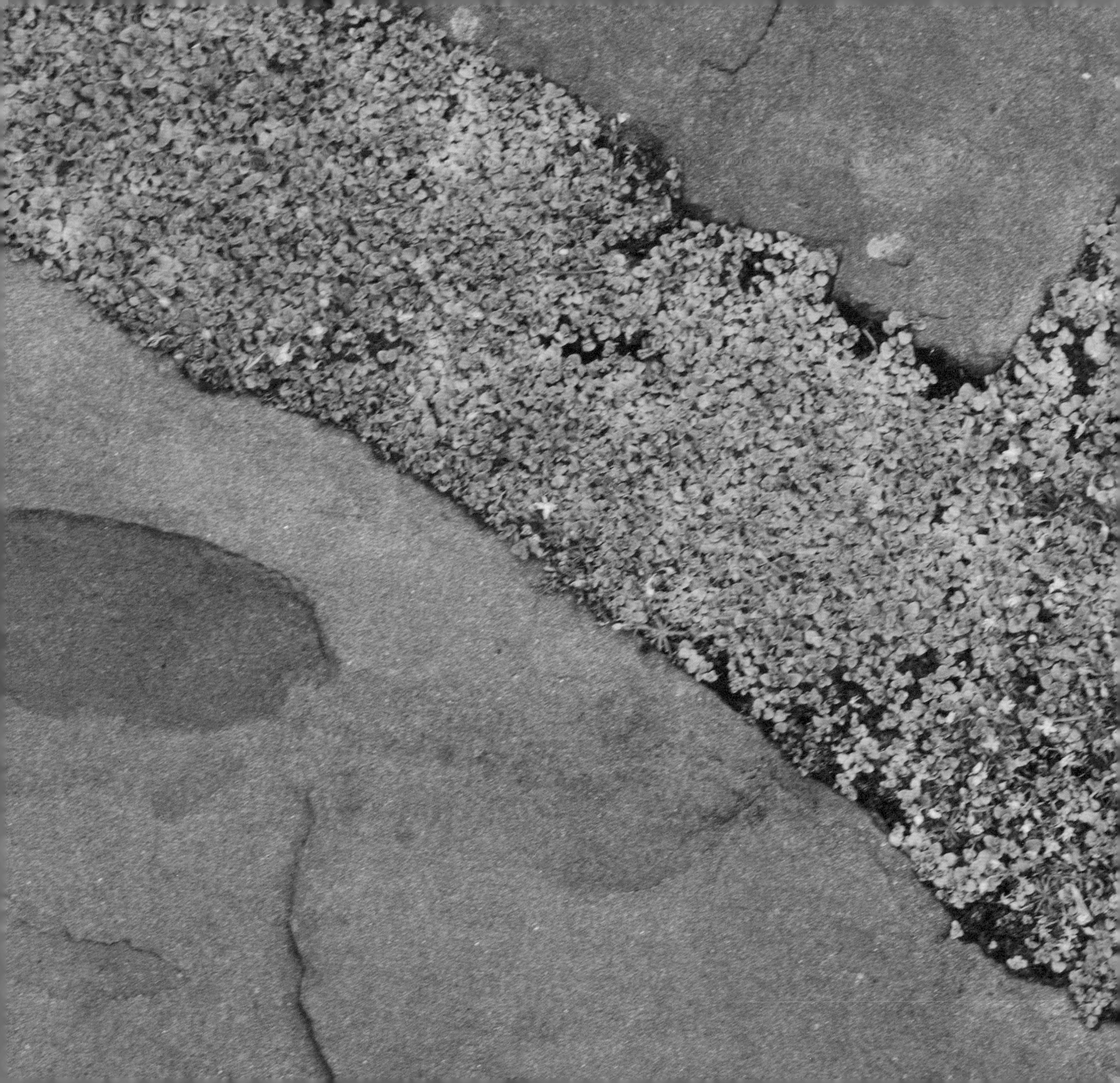